RETURN OF MAHA MAGHA: THE SACRED KUMBH OF THE SOUTH

Dr. C S Rayudu

Dr. C Subbarayudu

Title: Return of Maha Magha: The Sacred Kumbh of the South
Author: Dr. C. S. Rayudu
Publisher: Dr. C. Subbarayudu
Edition: First Edition
Year of Publication: 2026

This work is offered as a spiritual and cultural contribution, intended to inspire reflection, remembrance, and inner elevation. While every effort has been made to ensure accuracy and authenticity, the author and publisher assume no responsibility for errors, omissions, or consequences arising from the application or interpretation of the material herein. The concepts, narratives, rituals, and philosophical reflections presented in this book arise from the sacred streams of Advaita Vedānta and allied spiritual traditions and are shared with reverence and humility. Any resemblance to persons living or deceased—other than the saints, sages, and historical figures acknowledged—is purely coincidental.

ISBN: 978-93-5679-446-7
Cover Design & Illustrations: Sugun Cirigiri
Printed in: India
First Printing: January 2026

For permissions, inquiries, or spiritual dialogue, please contact:
Email: drcsrayudu@gmail.com

This book is dedicated to all those who have conceived, nurtured, and revived the sacred flame of Maha Magha—those who envisioned its return, organized its remembrance, and carried its spirit across time.

To the youth who embraced the call of dharma with courage;
to scholars who illumined its meaning with wisdom;
to sages and devotees who offered their hearts in surrender;
to institutions that preserved its traditions;
to the countless participants and promoters who became the living vessels of this sacred resurgence—
This work is for you.

And above all, I dedicate this offering to my beloved wife, Subhasini, whose unwavering presence, silent strength, and compassionate companionship have been the constant support in my spiritual journey. Her faith has been the wind beneath my wings, and her devotion the guiding light on every step of the path.

May 'Maha Magha' continue to flow through all of us,
as an enduring river of grace and remembrance.

CONTENTS

PREFACE

The Awakening of the Nila

Rivers are not merely bodies of water; they are the flowing veins of our civilization, carrying the memory of our ancestors and the vibration of our prayers. For over two and a half centuries, the sacred *Bharathapuzha*—our beloved *Nila*—flowed in silent longing, waiting for her children to return, waiting for the chants of the *Magha* month to rise once more from her sandy banks at *Thirunavaya*. That divine wait gives birth to this book, Return of Maha Magha: The Sacred Kumbh of the South. It is a chronicle of the resurrection.

Growing up in a small village, cradled by the spiritual stillness of the land, I was instinctively drawn to the unseen currents that bind Bharat into one sacred whole. From the ancient ghats of *Kāśī* to the forested ascent of Sabarimala, I sensed a single, unbroken spiritual energy flowing through the length and breadth of this land. Yet within this continuity lingered a quiet absence—a silence where the Kumbh of the South should have been. Why had *Mamankam*, once the luminous crown of Kerala's sacred calendar, receded into history and memory?

The answer came not in a library, but in the divine resolve of the *Sadhus* and *Acharyas* who decided that 2026 would be the year of awakening.

This work is structured around the momentous Maha Magha Mahotsavam held from January 18 to February 3, 2026. As you turn these pages, you are not just reading text; you are participating in a pilgrimage. I have endeavoured to capture the sanctity of the 17-day strict spiritual regimen, starting from the *Mauni Amavasya* on January 18th—a day of profound silence and the first holy dip—to the grand crescendo of the *Maha Magha Amritasnanam* on February 3rd.

In this book, I detail the revival of rituals that bridge the North and the South, symbolizing the unity of our Dharma. You will read of the *Nila Aarti*, where flames held by priests from Varanasi dance in rhythm with those from Kerala, creating a river of light that mirrors the sky. We explore the significance of the Dharma *Dhwajarohanam* (Flag Hoisting) on January 19th, marking the victory of spiritual persistence, and the celestial alignment of Ratha Saptami on January 25th, where the Sun God himself witnesses the devotion on the riverbanks.

I have also included the schedule of the *Mahameru Rath Yatra*, the arrival of the *Juna Akhara*, and the daily *Vedic Yagnas* intended to heal the scars of time. These events are not merely listed in a brochure; they represent the vitality of a thriving tradition being revived for the benefit of future generations.

This book is my offering—a *Pushpanjali*—at the feet of Sage Agastya and Lord *Navamukunda*. It is a guide for the devotee, a record for the historian, and a call to every Indian to recognize that the Ganges flows not just in the North, but wherever faith runs deep.

May the waters of the Nila purify your mind as you journey through these chapters.

Dr. C. S. Rayudu

Magha Masam, 2026

INTRODUCTION

The Silence of the River:

Rivers do not forget.
They remember even when civilizations fall silent.

This book, *Return of Maha Magha: The Sacred Kumbh of the South*, is born at a singular moment in time—January 19, 2026, on the sacred banks of the *Bharathapuzha*, revered in the spiritual imagination of Bharat as *Dakṣiṇa Gaṅgā*, the Southern Ganges. On this day, a flame was lit after a silence of two hundred and seventy years. That flame was not merely ceremonial. It marked the return of a memory that had waited patiently within the land, the river, and the collective unconscious of Kerala.

The Divine Nila: A Living Tīrtha:

The *Bharathapuzha*—called *Nila* by generations who lived with her rhythms—is not a river in the modern utilitarian sense. She is a *tīrtha*, a crossing point between the temporal and the eternal. Flowing from the *Sahyādri* ranges to the Arabian Sea, she has shaped Kerala's spiritual geography, cultural memory, poetry, ritual life, and sacred imagination. Saints walked her banks, kings sought legitimacy through her rites, ancestors were offered prayers to her waters, and *yajñas* once rose like columns of fire along her shores. To call her *Dakṣiṇa Gaṅgā* is not metaphorical reverence—it is civilizational recognition.

Yet for nearly three centuries, her banks remained ritually silent.

The 270-Year Slumber:

The last echoes of *Mamankam*—the great medieval congregation where *dharma, sovereignty, trade,* and *cosmic time* converged—faded in the late 18th century. Mysorean invasions, followed by colonial rule, dismantled not only political structures but ritual continuity itself. Sacred gatherings dissolved, temples retreated into survival mode, and collective rites gave way to private devotion. What was lost was not faith, but congregational memory.

Maha Magha did not vanish; it withdrew. It survived in palm-leaf manuscripts, oral traditions, temple lore, and in the silent patience of the river herself. This book begins by listening to that silence—not as absence, but as waiting.

Memory Beneath the Flow:

In Bharatiya thought, memory (*smṛti*) is not confined to texts or minds; it is embedded in *bhūmi*, in rivers, mountains, and sacred sites. Land remembers *yajñas* long after the flames have died. Water carries mantra vibrations long after chants have ceased. The Bharathapuzha remembered Maha Magha.

This work proceeds from the conviction that the 2026 revival was not an invention, imitation, or cultural reconstruction—but a realignment. Sacred time returned because sacred geography was ready to receive it again.

The Call of Return:

Why did Maha Magha seek rebirth in the 21st century? Because the modern world stands at a civilizational crossroads—ecological collapse, cultural amnesia, and spiritual fragmentation demand more than innovation; they demand remembrance. The return of Maha Magha answers a deeper hunger: for ritual intelligence, for sacred rhythm, for collective alignment with cosmic time.

This book situates the 2026 *Maha Magha Mahotsavam* not as an isolated festival but as a civilizational response to that call.

Purpose and Objectives of the Book:

The purpose of this book is fivefold and interwoven. It seeks to document the historical, mythological, and spiritual foundations of *Maha Magha* in Kerala, with *Thirunavaya* as its sacred axis; to recover the largely forgotten Southern traditions of *Magha, Kumbha*, and river-based congregational rites; to interpret *Maha Magha* through the lenses of cosmology, *jyotiṣa*, sacred geography, and ritual philosophy; to chronicle the 2026 revival not as an event but as a living civilizational moment, from collective *sankalpa* to the lighting of the First Flame; and finally, to offer a framework of stewardship that ensures continuity of sacred memory, preventing its reduction into mere spectacle.

Research Methodology:

The research for this book follows an interdisciplinary yet deeply dharmic methodology, weaving together multiple strands of knowledge and experience. It draws upon scriptural sources such as the *Purāṇas*, Smṛtis, *Itihāsa traditions*, *Kerala Tantra texts*, and *Jyotiṣa literature*, alongside *historical records* including temple chronicles, *Mamankam narratives*, *colonial accounts*, and *regional histories*. These textual foundations are complemented by oral traditions preserved by temple *priests, scholars, sādhus, elders,* and *living ritual lineages*, as well as direct field observation through first-hand witnessing of rituals, ceremonies, and pilgrim experiences during the 2026 Maha Magha Mahotsavam. Rituals are interpreted through a hermeneutic lens that understands them as symbolic and transformative actions rather than mere performances, and the entire study is grounded in an ecological-spiritual perspective that views river, land, and ritual as an integrated dharmic system. This holistic approach enables the book to function simultaneously as archive, narrative, and invocation.

Structure of the Book:

The book is structured in nine interlinked parts that together trace the journey of *Maha Magha* from remembrance to renewal. It begins by recovering the mythic, cosmic, and sacred geographic foundations of the tradition, then moves through the phases of historical loss, rupture, and eventual revival. From there, it enters the lived and experiential heart of Maha Magha through ritual, pilgrimage, and collective participation, before situating the Southern Kumbh within the wider spiritual and civilizational future of Bharat. The epilogue returns the reader to the *Bharathapuzha* itself—still flowing, still remembering, and silently awaiting humanity's continued responsibility to sacred time and sacred land.

A Threshold, Not a Chronicle:

This introduction does not invite the reader into a book alone. It invites them into a threshold. What follows is not merely history, theology, or reportage—but the story of how *smṛti* returned to *bhūmi*, how a river spoke after centuries of silence, and how a civilization remembered itself through fire, water, and collective will.

The Bharathapuzha still flows.
But now, she floats awake.

PROLOGUE

The First Flame: When Memory Returned to the River

On the sacred banks of the *Bharathapuzha*, where time does not march, but *circles back upon itself*, a flame was lit.

It was not merely fire that rose that morning—
It was remembrance.

January 19, 2026, will not endure as an ordinary date in the chronicles of Kerala. It will be recalled as a *threshold*—a moment when the visible world briefly parted to allow an older truth to step forward. On that day, at Thirunavaya, the First Flame Ceremony marked the return of *Maha Magha,* the ancient sacred congregation of the South. What unfolded was not the inauguration of a festival but the rekindling of a civilizational vow long held in silence.

For two hundred and seventy years, the *Bharathapuzha* had waited.

Not in emptiness—her waters never ceased to flow. She carried the red earth of the *Sahyadris*, the songs of farmers, the ashes of the departed, and the quiet prayers of those who still remembered her sanctity. Yet a deeper silence had settled upon her banks. The thunder of *Veda Ghoṣa*, once resonant during the *Mamankam* assemblies, had faded. The war drums of the *Zamorin* no longer rolled across the plains. The *Chāver* warriors had vanished into legend. And the month of Magha—once heavy with cosmic meaning—had thinned into a mere notation on the calendar.

Through invasion and erasure, through colonial order and modern indifference, the river endured. She endured as rivers do—not protesting, not pleading, but remembering. For she was never merely water. She was *Dakṣiṇa Gaṅgā*, the Southern embodiment of sacred flow, entrusted with holding time itself.

This morning, however, the air had a different density.

It was a Monday. Magha *Trayodaśī*. Before the sun crested the coconut palms of *Thirunavaya*, people began to arrive—not as spectators, not as tourists, but as pilgrims. Many could not articulate why they had come. They only knew they *had to*. Something dormant had stirred—an echo from within the collective memory of the land.

Uncertainty lingered in the cool mist. Only days earlier, bureaucratic obstacles and "stop memos" had threatened to extinguish the gathering before it could breathe. Skepticism hung heavy: *Can a tradition silenced for centuries truly return? Can memory outlive interruption?*

The answer revealed itself at eleven o'clock.

As the Governor of Kerala, Shri Rajendra Vishwanath Arlekar, stepped forward near the ancient *Navamukunda* Temple, the noise of the modern world seemed to retreat. Beside him stood *Mahamandaleśvar Swami Anandavanam Bhārati*—saffron-clad, unyielding, carrying in his stillness the resolve of generations that had refused to forget.

A match was struck. The flame touched the wick of the great *Nilavilakku*.

In that instant, something unseen was pierced. The trembling flame did more than illuminate a lamp—it tore through a veil that had covered the river for two hundred and seventy years. As the wick caught fire, a sound rose from the assembled thousands —not a cry of protest, but of release. It was the sound of a civilization exhaling after holding its breath for centuries.

As the *Dharma Dhvaja* unfurled and climbed the mast, the air filled once more with "*Om Namaḥ Śivāya*" and ancient Vedic mantras. The soil of *Thirunavaya*—long starved of these sounds —seemed to drink them in. What had been whispered in memory was now proclaimed aloud.

Yet the deepest transformation arrived at dusk.

As the sun dissolved into the horizon, staining the *Bharathapuzha* in violet and gold, the first *Nīlā Ārati* commenced. Heavy brass lamps were lifted by priests whose gestures carried both Kashi's ancient grace and Kerala's Tantric depth.

Fire met water.

Thousands of earthen lamps were set afloat, turning the river into a drifting constellation. The *Bharathapuzha*—spoken of in recent decades as a dying river—revealed herself instead as a living goddess, adorned in light. Elders wept, seeing with their own eyes what they had known only through fading stories. Children stood transfixed, witnessing the instant when heritage stepped out of textbooks and into breath.

The silence had been broken.
The river was awake.
Maha Magha had returned.

When the first bell echoed across the water, it announced not merely a festival but a declaration:

We are still here.

We remember.

This book is the story of that remembrance.

Thirunavaya: Where Time Bends into the Sacred:

Thirunavaya is no ordinary *tīrtha*. Known through centuries as Navayoga Kṣetra, it is believed to be a convergence not only of rivers but also of yogas, yugas, and yajñas. Kings have offered here, sages have lingered here, and pilgrims have dissolved their grief here. The land remembers what people often forget.

It was upon this consecrated soil that the First Flame was lit —declaring that Maha Magha's return to the South was not an imitation of northern grandeur, but a revelation rooted in Kerala's own sacred geometry.

The Flame as Witness:

In the Bharatiya spiritual vision, Agni is the first witness. Before speech, before vow, before law—fire is lit. The First Flame awakened *Agni* as *Sākṣī*, bearing testimony to a collective *saṅkalpa*: that *Maha Magha* would breathe again on the banks of the *Bharathapuzha*.

This was no decorative ritual. It was Agni remembered in his primal role—as messenger between earth and cosmos, purifier of intent, and illuminator of dharma. As the flame rose into the January sky, it seemed to echo the Puranic truth:

यत्र अग्निः, तत्र देवाः।

Yatra agniḥ, tatra devāḥ—
Where fire is present, the gods assemble.

A Southern Kumbh: Continuity, Not Replication:

This *Maha Magha* sought no replication of Prayagraj, Haridwar, or Ujjain. It announced something quieter and deeper: a *Southern Kumbh*, shaped by the rhythms of the *Sahyadris* and the land's spiritual temperament.

Maha Magha at Thirunavaya is not an imported memory. It is a restored inheritance. Sacred time does not belong to geography alone—it belongs to prepared consciousness. When a land remembers, the ritual returns.

Fire, River, and the Human Heart:

As the flame burned, the river flowed beside it—fire and water in eternal dialogue. One purifies through immersion; the other through illumination. Together, they formed the elemental axis of the Maha Magha Mahotsavam.

Those present did not merely witness the ceremony; they were entered by it. In the hush that followed, something rare emerged—a shared inwardness. The flame stood outside, but its true work had begun within.

A Flame That Must Travel Forward:

The First Flame was never meant to be extinguished with the ceremony's end. It is a living symbol—to be carried into homes and temples, into rivers and disciplines, into memory and action. It marks a journey toward sacred bathing, inner purification, charity, dialogue, and continuity.

January 19, 2026, stands as the moment when Kerala reclaimed her place in the pan-Indian rhythm of Maha Magha—not through spectacle, but through sincerity.

Long after the chants faded and the lamps dimmed, the Bharathapuzha continued to flow—as she always has. Yet something had changed. She had been reminded of herself—not merely as a river, but as a tīrtha of time.

When Smṛti Returns to Bhūmi:

Maha Magha returned not as a spectacle but as *smṛti*—ancient memory re-entering living land. At *Thirunavaya*, soil, river, and flame remembered their sacred rhythm. The South's Kumbh reawakened the alignment of time, intention, and geography, transforming revival into responsibility and remembrance into stewardship.

The First Flame had spoken. And in its quiet radiance, it whispered a promise:

Maha Magha has returned.

The South is ready.

PART I

THE ANCIENT ECHOES
Myth, Memory, and the First Sacred Fires

CHAPTER 1: PARASHURĀMA'S YAJÑA AT THIRUNAVAYA

Ancient echoes, such as myths, memories, and the first sacred fires, open a doorway into humanity's earliest spiritual consciousness. Long before history was written, myths carried truth, memory shaped identity, and fire became the first sacred witness to human aspiration. This section explores how ancient narratives preserved cosmic order, moral law, and collective wisdom, transmitting dharma through symbol and ritual. The first sacred fires were not merely sources of warmth but altars of transformation—linking earth and sky, mortals and the eternal. In these echoes of the past, we discover the primal roots of faith, culture, and humanity's enduring quest for meaning.

1. The Creation of Kerala and the Consecration of the Land

In the deep time of *Bharata's* sacred memory, before kingdoms hardened into borders and rivers bore names of convenience, the western edge of the subcontinent lay submerged beneath restless waters. It was *Parashurāma*—the sixth *avatāra* of Lord Viṣṇu, bearer of the axe and restorer of dharma—who altered the destiny of this land. As the *Purāṇas* recount, *Parashurāma* reclaimed Kerala from the sea, commanding the waters to retreat and reveal fertile earth sanctified for tapas and *yajña*.

Paraśurāma and the Command to the Ocean:

Having fulfilled his fearsome vow and laid down his axe, Paraśurāma turned from conquest to atonement. Seeking a land where *tapas, yajña,* and *brahmavidyā* could flourish unbroken, he stood upon the western edge of *Bhārata,* facing the roaring ocean. The Purāṇas describe the sea as restless, encroaching, and untamed—symbolic of unrestrained time and desire.

Raising his divine axe, *Paraśurāma* invoked his inner resolve and uttered the command of dharma. The waters, bound by cosmic law, obeyed.

आपो हि धर्मस्य वशा भवन्ति

Aapo hi dharmasya vashā bhavanti

"Even the waters move under the command of dharma."

With a thunderous retreat, the sea withdrew, revealing a long crescent of fertile land—fresh, unsullied, and waiting for consecration. This was *Keralam*, not merely reclaimed earth, but **भूमि-यज्ञफलम्** *Bhūmi–yajña-phalam* —the fruit of a cosmic sacrifice.

The Land Sanctified for Tapas and Yajña:

The newly revealed land was not handed to kings or conquerors. *Paraśurāma* envisioned Kerala as a **क्षेत्रं ब्रह्मविद्यायाः** *Kṣetraṁ brahmavidyāyāḥ* —a field for spiritual knowledge. He invited sages, priests, and householders committed to dharma, assigning lands for temples, hermitages, and sacred groves.

The *Purāṇas* declare that rivers were summoned, mountains were stabilized, and forests were blessed so that *ṛta*, the cosmic order, could settle permanently into the landscape.
यत्र तपः स्थिरं, तत्र देवाः वसन्ति

Yatra tapaḥ sthiraṁ, tatra devāḥ vasanti

"Where austerity stands firm, there the gods abide."

Kerala was thus conceived not as a kingdom of power, but as a land of restraint, where life would move in rhythm with nature—where rain, river, ritual, and reflection would form a single continuum.

Waters That Obeyed Consciousness:

The retreat of the sea was not an act of domination but of alignment. *Paraśurāma* did not conquer nature; he reordered it. In Dharmic thought, nature resists greed but responds to consciousness. The ocean withdrew because the command arose not from ego, but from cosmic responsibility.

यदा चेतना शुद्धा, तदा प्रकृतिः अनुगच्छति

Yadā cetanā śuddhā, tadā prakṛtiḥ anugacchati

"When consciousness is pure, nature follows."

Thus, Kerala emerged as a living testament to this principle—a land where water did not merely irrigate fields but remembered obedience to sacred intent.

Kerala as a Living Yajña:

In this epic vision, Kerala itself becomes a perpetual *yajña*. The mountains are its altars, the rivers its oblations, the monsoon its sacred fire, and human life its offering. Bharathapuzha (Nila), flowing through this reclaimed land, carries this primal memory—of waters that once parted in reverence and now flow in service.

भूमिर्देवी, जलं प्राणः, कर्म यज्ञः

"The earth is divine, water is life, and action is sacrifice."

A Land Born of Command and Compassion:

The *Purāṇic* account of *Paraśurāma* reclaiming Kerala from the sea is not a legend to be read lightly. It is a civilizational metaphor: when violence is renounced, creation begins; when power bows to penance, land itself becomes sacred.

Kerala, in this telling, is not merely a coastal strip—it is consciousness made terrain, a land where the sea once listened, and where even today, rivers flow as though remembering the command of a sage who sought not dominion, but dharma.

The creation, in the *Bharatiya* cosmology, is never complete without consecration. Land is not merely uncovered; it must be awakened. Thus, Kerala was not only formed—it was ritually *invoked* into sacred order. The soil that emerged was not inert geography but *bhūmi* charged with *ṛta*, the cosmic law spoken of in the *Ṛg Veda*. *Parashurāma's* act was not conquest over nature, but alignment with it—restoring harmony between human intention and cosmic rhythm.

2. The First Yajña on the Banks of the Nila

Upon this newly revealed land flowed the *Bharathapuzha*—later revered as *Nila*—gentle in movement yet profound in presence. Recognizing her as a vessel of sacred continuity, *Parashurāma* chose her banks at *Thirunavaya* to kindle the first *yajña* of Kerala. Fire was lit, not merely to burn offerings, but to establish *Agni* as *sākṣī*, the eternal witness between heaven and earth.

The Vedas proclaim, *"Agnim īḷe purohitam"—Agni* is the first priest, the bridge between mortals and the divine. In lighting the sacred fire at *Thirunavaya, Parashurāma* anchored Kerala into the Vedic universe itself. This *yajña* aligned *deśa (space), kāla (time), and karma (action),* establishing the land as fit for dharmic life. The river bore the chants, the sky received the smoke, and the earth absorbed the merit. This was not a local rite. It was a civilisational ignition.

3. Invocation of the Trimūrti

Unlike ordinary sacrificial rites, the *yajña* at *Thirunavaya* carried a rare invocation—the conscious calling of the *Trimūrti*: *Brahmā* the creator, *Viṣṇu* the preserver, and *Śiva* the dissolver. *Purāṇic* tradition holds that all three presences were invoked to sanctify the land in totality—birth, sustenance, and transcendence.

Brahmā was invoked to stabilize creation upon reclaimed earth. *Viṣṇu*, *Parashurāma's* own cosmic source, was invoked to sustain dharma across ages. Śiva was called to anchor renunciation, tapas, and liberation. Thus, *Thirunavaya* was not consecrated for prosperity alone, but for *mokṣa*. This triadic invocation transformed the region into a living mandala—where life could flourish without losing sight of transcendence.

4. Thirunavaya as Navayoga Kṣetra

From this *yajña* emerged the identity of *Thirunavaya* as *Navayoga Kṣetra*—a sacred field where nine yogic streams converge. *Yoga* here does not refer merely to bodily discipline but to pathways of union: *bhakti (*devotion*), jñāna (*knowledge (spiritual wisdom)*), karma (*Action and its consequences*), tapas (*austerity / spiritual discipline*), mantra (*sacred sound*), dhyana (*meditation*), yajna (*sacrifice / sacred ritual*), tyāga (*renunciation*),* and *anugraha (*divine grace / blessing*).* The land itself became a yogic instrument.

The Vedāṅgic order—*śikṣā (*phonetics / pronunciation (the study of sound and speech)*), chandas (*prosody / poetics (the study of meter and poetic rhythm)*), vyākaraṇa (*grammar (sanskrit grammar and linguistic structure)*), nirukta (*etymology / explanation of meanings (study of word origins)*), kalpa (*ritual science / vedic rites and procedures), and *jyotiṣa* (astrology / astronomical knowledge (science of celestial bodies))—found natural expression here, as ritual, language, timekeeping, and meaning aligned effortlessly with place. *Thirunavaya* thus became a *tīrtha of time*, where past, present, and future touched.

It is from this primordial consecration that all later gatherings —*Mamankam, Maha Magha*, and the returning Kumbh of the South—draw their legitimacy. When fire is lit at *Thirunavaya* today, it is not innovation. It is remembrance.

The ancient echoes never faded. They only waited to be heard again.

CHAPTER 2: MĀMĀṄKAM—WHEN DHARMA, SOVEREIGNTY, AND TIME CONVERGED

The Sacred Reckoning: Where Power Bowed Before Kāla

1. Māmāṅkam as Ritual, Royal, and Civilizational Gathering

In the sacred cartography of *Bhārata*, some *tīrthas* cleanse the body, some illumine the mind, and some awaken remembrance across ages. *Māmāṅkam* belonged to the last category. It was not merely a royal assembly nor a public congregation—it was a civilizational rite, where polity, piety, and cosmic rhythm aligned.

Held once every twelve solar years on the hallowed banks of the Nila, *Māmāṅkam* unfolded as a *Mahāyajña of Kāla*. Kings, traders, pilgrims, sages, and warriors gathered not only in space but also in shared submission to time. Here, history paused to listen to eternity.

कालो हि दुरतिक्रमः
Kālo hi duratikramaḥ
Time is inexorable; none may transgress its command.
— *Mahābhārata, Vana Parva*

At *Māmāṅkam*, time did not merely flow. *Time revealed its verdict.*

2. Trade, Pilgrimage, and Cosmic Timing

Māmāṅkam was also a living confluence of worlds. Trade routes converged with pilgrimage paths; material exchange unfolded alongside spiritual seeking. Merchants arrived with spices and silks, pilgrims with vows and prayers, and ascetics with silence sharpened by tapas.

Yet none arrived by chance. The gathering was governed by *jyotiṣa*, aligned to celestial cycles that echoed the twelve-year rhythm sacred to Jupiter and destiny alike. Commerce found legitimacy through dharma, and pilgrimage found grounding through daily life. Thus, prosperity was not opposed to spirituality—it was consecrated by it.

3. The Zamorin, Sovereignty, and Sacred Legitimacy

The *Samoothiri* of Kozhikode presided over *Māmāṅkam* not as an absolute monarch, but as a trustee of sacred order. His authority was ritual, not personal, temporal, not eternal. He stood as the visible axis of governance, yet always beneath the unseen sovereignty of *Kāla*.

Purāṇic memory recalls Māmāṅkam as a rite where *rājya bowed to ṛta*—where power sought renewal only by acknowledging impermanence.

न राज्यं न च सौख्यं हि

न च प्राणाः स्थिरा नृणाम् ।

कालेन सर्वं हर्येत

कः स्थास्यति सनातनः ॥

na rājyaṁ na ca saukhyaṁ hi

na ca prāṇāḥ sthirā nṛṇām |

kālena sarvaṁ haryeta

kaḥ sthāsyati sanātanaḥ ||

Neither kingdom, nor pleasure, nor even life endures.

Time consumes all—who may claim permanence?

Thus, Māmāṅkam reminded ruler and subject alike: *Sovereignty survives only when aligned with dharma.*

From Harmony to Conflict

4. Chāver Warriors and Ritualized Sacrifice

As centuries turned, the inner harmony of Māmāṅkam slowly absorbed the weight of human ambition. From this tension emerged the Chāver—warriors bound by vow, not rage, by renunciation, not hatred. Their act was not personal violence but ritual extremity, shaped by an age that expressed sacrifice through the body itself. In Vedic vision, sacrifice sustains order.

यज्ञो वै विष्णुः
Yajño vai Viṣṇuḥ
Sacrifice itself is Viṣṇu.

—*Śatapatha Brāhmaṇa*

The Chāver offered their lives as oblation, believing that through supreme tyāga, the moral gravity of kingship would be preserved. Their destiny, though tragic in form, belonged to a worldview where life itself was an offering.

5. Māmāṅkam as Political Tapas

Unlike coronations guarded by ceremony and shield, Māmāṅkam exposed rulership to uncertainty. To govern was to stand unarmoured before destiny. This was political tapas—authority refined by the constant nearness of mortality.

न तपो विद्यते क्षत्रे

न तपो राज्यधारणे

na tapo vidyate kṣatre

na tapo rājya-dhāraṇe

There is no greater austerity (*tapas*) for a *Kshatriya*, and no greater penance than the burden of ruling a kingdom. Thus, cowardice could find no refuge in ritual. Only one who accepted impermanence could claim the right to govern others who lived beneath its shadow.

6. Kāla, Agni, and the River Nila

The sanctity of *Māmāṅkam* rested upon a sacred triad:

1. *Nila*, bearer of ancestral memory

2. *Agni*, eternal witness to vows

3. *Kāla*, the unseen governor of all cycles

नदीनां पावनं तीर्थं

अग्निः साक्षी महान् स्मृतः ।

कालः सर्वस्य नियन्ता

त्रयं यत्र समागतम् ॥

nadīnāṁ pāvanaṁ tīrthaṁ

agniḥ sākṣī mahān smṛtaḥ |

kālaḥ sarvasya niyantā

trayaṁ yatra samāgatam ||

The river is the purifying sacred place (*tīrtha*),
Fire is the great witness (*sākṣī*),
Time is the controller of all,
Where these three come together.

Māmāṅkam was such a convergence—where earth remembered, fire affirmed, and time completed its measure.

7. The Long Silence and the Waiting Memory

With the arrival of colonial modernity, Māmāṅkam was misunderstood. Its ritual depth was reduced to spectacle, its spiritual intent to disorder. The fires were extinguished; the cycle was interrupted.

Yet *smṛti* does not vanish.

नष्टोऽपि संस्कृतो धर्मः

कालान्तरे पुनर्भवेत्

naṣṭo'pi saṃskṛto dharmaḥ

kālāntare punar bhavet

Even if Dharma is lost, it is sanctified again in another age. What followed was not death, but *pralaya*—a sacred pause before renewal.

8. From Māmāṅkam to Mahā Māgha: When Spiritual Congregation Absorbed Martial Destiny

What *Māmāṅkam* once enacted through the language of kings and warriors, *Mahā Māgha* now reclaims through water, fire, and collective remembrance. The centre shifts—from sovereignty to sanctity, from bodily sacrifice to inner offering.

यत्र स्मृतिः, तत्र तीर्थम्

yatra smṛtiḥ, tatra tīrtham

Where memory (*smṛti*) resides, there is a sacred place (*tīrtha*).

The blade yields to the flame.
The battlefield dissolves into the bathing ghat.
The vow of death transforms into a vow of awakening.

Mahā Māgha does not erase *Māmāṅkam*. It fulfils it.

Closing Cadence

Thus stands Māmāṅkam—
not as a relic of conflict,
but as a syllable in Kerala's eternal mantra.

Time spoke.

Power listened.
Memory endured.

And when the fires of *Mahā Māgha* rise again at *Thirunavaya*,
The river remembers.
the land responds,
and *Kāla*—
ancient, patient, and awake—
allows the echo to return as light.

CHAPTER 3: THE LOST SANCTITY (1766 CE)

When Fire Was Silenced and Memory Was Buried

I. The Shattered Rhythm of Dharma

Sacred geographies do not perish easily. They erode—slowly, painfully—when time turns hostile and power forgets reverence. The year 1766 CE stands in Kerala's spiritual memory as a deep fissure in sacred time. It was not merely an invasion of territory but an invasion of *ṛta*—the cosmic rhythm that once governed land, ritual, and remembrance. What was ruptured was not stone alone, but continuity.

न राज्यं न च सौख्यं हि

न च प्राणाः स्थिरा नृणाम् ।

कालेन सर्वं हर्येत

कः स्थास्यति सनातनः ॥

Na rājyaṁ na ca saukhyaṁ hi

na ca prāṇāḥ sthirā nṛṇām |

kālena sarvaṁ haryeta

kaḥ sthāsyati sanātanaḥ ||

Neither kingdom nor comfort, nor even life itself is permanent.

Time consumes all—who alone stands eternal?

Yet even Time, when misaligned with dharma, leaves wounds that echo across centuries.

II. Mysorean Invasions and the Rupture of Ritual

When Power Displaced the Sacred

The Mysorean incursions into Malabar in the latter half of the eighteenth century marked a decisive turning point—not only in political history but also in the spiritual destiny of the land. The imperatives of imperial expansion, military consolidation, and revenue control drove these campaigns, initially led by Hyder Ali and later by Tipu Sultan. Yet, as so often in history, the sacred lay directly in the path of power.

Sacred sites, though intrinsically neutral to politics, are never neutral to civilization. Temples, *yajña*-grounds, riverside *kṣetras*, and ritual assemblies are the invisible infrastructure of a culture. When armies move, it is this invisible order that fractures first. In Malabar, temples were dismantled or repurposed, priestly families were displaced, and the continuity of daily, seasonal, and epochal rituals was violently interrupted. What broke was not merely architecture, but time itself.

At *Thirunavaya*, the rupture was especially profound. This was not an ordinary temple town; it was a *ritual axis*, a place where fire, water, mantra, and cosmic timing had once converged seamlessly. Here, *yajñas* had been performed not as episodic events, but as civilizational affirmations—renewing the bond between land (*bhūmi*), people, and cosmic law (*ṛta*). When the Mysorean advance unsettled the region, these *yajñas* fell silent.

The Bharathapuzha (Nila) continued to flow, indifferent in

appearance yet burdened with loss. Rivers remember. Her banks, once alive with Vedic chant, invocation, and sacrificial cadence, echoed instead with absence. The silence was not natural; it was historical. The sacred had not disappeared—it had been forced out of place.

This distinction is crucial. The sanctity of *Thirunavaya* was not annihilated; it was dislocated. Priests fled to safer regions, carrying fragments of memory but unable to sustain full ritual cycles. Palm-leaf manuscripts—repositories of mantras, kalpas, genealogies, and ritual timings—were lost, destroyed, or scattered. Even more fragile were the oral lineages, where intonation, sequence, and subtle meaning were preserved not in text, but in living voices. When those voices were silenced or dispersed, an entire epistemology collapsed.

अग्निः साक्षी महान् स्मृतः

Agniḥ sākṣī mahān smṛtaḥ

Agni is remembered as the outstanding witness.

When Agni is extinguished, it is not the flame that dies—it is testimony itself. When Agni no longer burns in a consecrated space, the witness withdraws—not in anger, but in waiting. Ritual requires stability: of place, of community, of rhythm. War dissolves all three simultaneously.

The Mysorean invasions thus represent more than a chapter of military history. They mark a rupture in ritual time—a moment when sacred continuity was broken so abruptly that restoration itself became uncertain. Festivals dependent on precise astronomical alignment, collective memory, and uninterrupted lineage—such as *Maha Magha*—could not survive such a fracture. Without custodians, calendars, and collective participation, cosmic time lost its earthly anchor.

What followed was not immediate forgetting but gradual

erosion. A generation without ritual becomes a culture without reference points. Sacred memory, once embodied in action, was reduced to fragments—stories without enactment, places without practice.

Yet even here, dharma does not concede defeat.

नष्टोऽपि संस्कृतो धर्मः

कालान्तरे पुनर्भवेत्

Naṣṭo'pi saṁskṛto dharmaḥ

kālāntare punarbhavet

Even when refined dharma is lost, it re-emerges in another age.

The rupture caused by the Mysorean invasions was real and devastating—but it was not final. Beneath silence, the old fires waited. The land remembered what power could not erase.

This rupture marked the first major desacralization of Maha Magha, not by denial, but by enforced forgetting. The ritual clock of Kerala was broken.

III. From Invasion to Amnesia: The End of Sacred Time

If invasion wounded the body of the land, colonial modernity numbed its soul. British administration brought with it cartography, census, revenue codes, and rational order—tools of governance that knew territory but not *tīrtha*, land but not *kṣetra*.

Sacred geography was flattened into neutral space. Rivers became "water resources," temples "structures," and festivals "local customs." What could not be measured was dismissed. What could not be taxed was ignored.

यत्र स्मृतिः, तत्र तीर्थम्

Yatra smṛtiḥ, tatra tīrtham

Where memory abides, there is a sacred crossing.

Colonial modernity did not destroy *Thirunavaya*—it displaced memory from it. The land remained, but its soul was unrecorded.

IV. Desacralization Without Destruction

Unlike earlier invasions, colonial rule did not violently suppress ritual everywhere. Instead, it rendered ritual irrelevant. Sacred time was replaced by administrative calendars. Cyclical festivals gave way to linear progress. *Maha Magha*—once a convergence of cosmic time—found no place in gazettes or legal registers.

कालः सर्वस्य नियन्ता

Kālaḥ sarvasya niyantā

Time is the regulator of all.

But this new time was not *kāla* as understood by the sages—it was mechanical, external, and desacralized. Thus, sanctity was not lost in fire or blood but buried beneath paperwork.

V. The Burial of Maha Magha Beneath Political History

As centuries passed, *Maha Magha* faded from living practice to fragmentary memory. *Mamankam* survived—because it aligned with political narratives of power and spectacle. *Maha Magha* did not—because it belonged to cosmic time, not royal chronicle.

It became a footnote, then a silence.

नष्टोऽपि संस्कृतो धर्मः

कालान्तरे पुनर्भवेत्

Naṣṭo'pi saṁskṛto dharmaḥ

kālāntare punarbhavet

Even when refined dharma is lost, it shall arise again in another age.

Maha Magha was not abolished. It was entombed—beneath invasions, beneath modernity, beneath the tyranny of recorded history.

VI. Silence Is Not Absence

The sacred does not vanish. It waits. Beneath *Thirunavaya's* soil, beneath the quiet banks of the *Nila*, the old alignments still endure. Fire remembers where it once burned. Water remembers the *mantras* it once carried. Time itself remembers its rupture.

This chapter is not an elegy. It is a recognition. For when memory stirs, sanctity returns—not as nostalgia, but as renewal.

The lost sanctity was never destroyed. It was only unheard. And what was once unheard,
It may yet be invoked again.

PART II

THE COSMIC ORIGINS OF MAHA MAGHA When Time Becomes Sacred

CHAPTER 4: SAMUDRA MANTHANA—THE BIRTH OF SACRED TIME

Maha Magha

Maha Magha is not merely a festival marked by ritual observance; it is a profound cosmic moment when time itself turns sacred. Rooted in celestial alignments and ancient dharmic wisdom, Maha Magha represents the confluence of cosmic order, human consciousness, and sacred geography. As the Sun enters *Magha Nakshatra*, time is believed to open a luminous threshold where ancestral memory, karmic purification, and divine grace intersect. Rivers become vessels of liberation, actions acquire timeless potency, and the ordinary dissolves into the eternal. Maha Magha reminds humanity that sacredness is not confined to space alone—it unfolds when time awakens to divinity.

Samudra Manthana

In the beginning, time was not counted—it was experienced. It breathed with the cosmos, moved with the stars, and revealed itself through divine events. Among these events, none is more primordial, more civilizational decisive, than *Samudra Manthana*—the churning of the cosmic ocean. This was not merely a mythic struggle between devas and asuras; it was the moment when sacred time was born, when eternity fractured itself into cycles that humanity could enter, honour, and align with.

1. Amṛta, Kalaśa, Devas, and Asuras

The Samudra Manthana unfolds at a time when the balance of the cosmos trembles. The devas, custodians of *ṛta*—the cosmic order—are weakened, their vitality diminished by the curse of time itself. The *asuras*, embodiments of raw power and ambition, surge forward. Neither light nor shadow can prevail alone. Thus, *Vishnu*, the Preserver, orchestrates a paradox: *devas* and *asuras* must churn together.

Mount Mandara becomes the axis of existence, *Vasuki* the serpent the living rope, and the Milky Ocean the womb of creation. What emerges from this churning is not immediately nectar, but terror and wonder—*Hālāhala*, the poison of accumulated time, threatening to dissolve creation. Shiva consumes it, holding death itself at his throat, reminding the cosmos that sacrifice precedes immortality.

Only after this purgation does *Amṛta* arise—the nectar of immortality—contained within the *kalaśa*, the sacred vessel. The *kalaśa* is not just a pot; it is a symbol of time held in form, eternity made accessible. When *Vishnu*, as *Mohini*, carries the *Amṛta* away, drops spill across the earth and heavens. These drops sanctify locations and moments forever. Where *Amṛta* falls, time itself becomes holy.

2. The Cosmic Origin of Kumbh

The *Kumbh* is not a festival created by society; it is society remembering a cosmic event. The places where *Amṛta* touched the earth—*Prayagraj, Haridwar, Ujjain,* and *Nashik*—became *tīrthas*, not because of geography alone, but because cosmic time imprinted itself upon them.

Kumbh occurs not annually, but rhythmically, governed by Jupiter, the Sun, the Moon, and their intricate celestial dance. This is crucial: sacredness is not static. It returns. It pulses. It waits. When the planetary alignments recreate the original cosmic moment, the gates of time reopen. What once happened in myth becomes available again in lived reality.

During Kumbh, rivers do not merely flow with water; they flow with cosmic memory. A dip is not symbolic—it is participatory. The pilgrim enters the same stream of time that the *devas* once entered. Bathing becomes an act of alignment, where personal *karma* is momentarily suspended within a larger cosmic rhythm.

Thus, Kumbh is Samudra Manthana reenacted on earth—a collective churning of humanity seeking renewal.

3. Sacred Time Cycles as Civilizational Intelligence

Ancient civilizations did not ask, "What is the date?" It asked, "What is the quality of this moment?" Sacred time cycles —*Kumbh, Maha Magha*, eclipses, solstices—are expressions of a profound civilizational intelligence that understood time as alive.

These cycles served as

1. Moral regulators, reminding societies to pause, purify, and realign.

2. Psychological resets, dissolving accumulated fear and fatigue.

3. Spiritual technologies, allowing ordinary humans access to extraordinary states.

Unlike linear time, which exhausts, sacred time renews. It does not push humanity forward blindly; it draws people inward, back to the source. The repetition of sacred cycles ensured continuity across generations, anchoring society not in power or conquest, but in remembrance.

In this vision, time is not an enemy that steals life—it is a teacher that returns grace.

The Birth of Sacred Time:

Samudra Manthana teaches that immortality is not a one-time gift, but a re-entry through awareness. *Amṛta* still flows, not in oceans, but in moments when humanity aligns with cosmic order. Sacred time is the bridge between myth and memory, eternity and everyday life.

When humanity remembers how to churn its own inner ocean —between fear and faith, desire and discipline—the *kalaśa* reappears.

And time, once again, becomes sacred.

CHAPTER 5: MAGHA MĀSA—THE MONTH OF DIVINE DESCENT

Magha Māsa is not merely a division of the lunar calendar; it is a descent of sacred time into human life. When the Sun journeys through *Makara* and the Moon graces *Magha Nakṣatra*, the cosmos enters a state of heightened receptivity. The *Purāṇas* proclaim that during *Magha*, *dharma* walks the earth in visible form, rivers awaken with salvific power, and even the gods incline themselves toward human prayer. This period is the month when heaven leans closer to earth, inviting humanity into conscious alignment with cosmic order.

1. Magha in Purāṇas and Smṛtis: Scriptural Foundations of Sacred Time

The sanctity of *Magha Māsa* occupies a unique and exalted position in India's sacred literature. Across the *Purāṇas* and *Smṛtis*, *Magha* is not treated as a routine calendrical period but as a divinely charged interval of time, deliberately instituted by cosmic law for the upliftment of humanity. The repeated and emphatic glorification of Magha in texts such as the *Padma Purāṇa, Skanda Purāṇa, Bhaviṣya Purāṇa,* and *Nārada Smṛti* signals its exceptional status among all months. These scriptures affirm that during Magha, time itself becomes an instrument of grace, amplifying the spiritual consequences of even the simplest righteous act.

The *Purāṇas* repeatedly assert that a single act of virtue performed in Magha—be it a bath, a prayer, or an offering—yields merit multiplied manifold, often equated with the fruits of prolonged penance undertaken across several lifetimes. This is not mere praise but a theological statement: Magha signifies a significant reduction in the resistance between human effort and divine response. Spiritual progress requires intense exertion; in Magha, the cosmos itself assists the seeker.

A recurring *Purāṇic* motif describes *Lord Viṣṇu* dwelling in sacred waters during *Magha Māsa*. Rivers, confluences, lakes, and seas are thus transformed into living sanctuaries. Viṣṇu's presence signifies preservation and restoration—suggesting that Magha is designed to heal the fractures caused by accumulated *karma*. Alongside *Viṣṇu*, the *Devas* are said to assemble invisibly at *tīrthas*, observing and bearing witness to human observance. The pilgrim, though unaware, is never alone; every act is performed in a cosmic audience.

The *Smṛti* texts provide the practical architecture of Magha observance. They prescribe *brahma-muhūrta snāna*, sensory restraint, simplicity of living, charitable giving, and remembrance of ancestors. Importantly, these injunctions are not framed as optional acts of piety but as components of a holistic spiritual discipline. Magha, therefore, is not about performing a single ritual for merit; it is about temporarily reorganizing one's entire mode of life in alignment with dharma.

In several *Smṛtis*, *Magha* is likened to a *mahā-vrata*, a powerful practice accessible to all—householders, ascetics, kings, and commoners alike. Magha incorporates spiritual intensity into daily life, unlike severe austerities that require giving up worldly responsibilities. It allows society as a whole to pause, purify, and recalibrate itself annually, ensuring civilizational continuity through shared sacred rhythm.

The scriptures further elevate Magha by describing it as a cosmic *yāga*—a universal sacrifice unfolding across time rather than space. In this *yāga*, the human body becomes the altar, breath becomes the sacred fire, and intention becomes the oblation, discipline becomes the sacred fire, and intention becomes the mantra. The practitioner does not merely observe the sacrifice; he or she becomes the sacrifice. This imagery reveals a profound metaphysical insight: liberation is not achieved by escaping life, but by consecrating it.

Most significantly, the *Purāṇas* explain that *Magha Māsa* was instituted to cleanse deep-seated karmic residues that remain untouched by ordinary rituals and moral living. Certain impressions, accumulated over births, require not effort alone but auspicious time for their dissolution. Magha provides this opening. It is time designed not to measure life, but to redeem it.

Thus, within the *Purāṇic* and *Smṛti* vision, *Magha Māsa* stands as sacred time par excellence—a compassionate interruption in the flow of ordinary existence, where cosmic law bends toward mercy and offers humanity a recurring chance at renewal, remembrance, and release.

2. The Superiority of Magha Among Months: Why Time Itself Bows

Among the twelve lunar months, *Magha Māsa* is repeatedly acclaimed in the *Purāṇas* as *śreṣṭha*—the most exalted, the most potent, and the most compassionate. This supremacy is expressed through powerful analogies: just as the *Ganga* sanctifies all rivers, *Viṣṇu* embodies the essence of all deities, and the cow sustains life through silent generosity, Magha stands above all months as the very embodiment of sacred time. Such comparisons are not poetic excess; they reveal a metaphysical hierarchy in which time itself possesses varying qualities and capacities.

The superiority of Magha does not arise from human preference or ritual convention. It is rooted in cosmic alignment. Following *Makara Saṅkrānti*, the Sun begins its northward journey (*uttarāyaṇa*), a movement traditionally associated with illumination, ascent, and spiritual clarity. Solar energy, having completed its transition, attains stability and benevolence. Simultaneously, the Moon traverses' phases that resonate deeply with the *pitṛ-loka*, the ancestral realm. This dual harmony creates a rare and bright balance between *sūrya-tattva*, which is the principle of consciousness and awakening, and *chandra-tattva*, which is the principle of memory, emotion, and continuity.

In ordinary time, these two forces often pull in opposite directions—illumination without memory becomes arrogance, while memory without illumination becomes inertia. Magha reconciles them. The human mind, ordinarily fragmented by desire and distraction, becomes naturally receptive to *saṃyama*—restraint, reflection, and inwardness. This aspect is why disciplines that feel arduous in other months unfold with surprising ease in Magha. The struggle lessens not because effort disappears, but because time itself cooperates.

Scriptural tradition makes a striking declaration: in other months, the seeker must ascend toward the gods through strenuous practice, but in Magha, the gods descend. The distance between the human and the divine contracts. Devotion performed in this month does not travel upward through layers of resistance; it is received directly, as though the heavens lean closer to earth. This concept is the theological basis for the belief that Magha multiplies merit beyond measure.

One of the most compassionate dimensions of Magha's

superiority is its inclusivity. Ascetic disciplines are often inaccessible to householders burdened by social and familial responsibilities. *Magha* dissolves this divide. A simple dawn bath, a humble act of charity, or a moment of sincere remembrance performed by a householder during *Magha* is equated with severe penances undertaken in solitude. In this month, the spiritual field is levelled; grace does not discriminate.

The *Purāṇas* further suggest that Magha was ordained precisely for those unable to renounce the world. It is time that compensates for human limitation. Where personal capacity ends, sacred time begins its work. Thus, Magha becomes a democratization of liberation, offering spiritual access not through withdrawal from life, but through conscious participation in it.

Ultimately, *Magha Māsa* teaches a profound truth: time is not uniform. Just as soil differs in fertility and seasons differ in yield, moments differ in spiritual potency. Some moments merely pass, others open. Magha is such an opening—a door in time through which humanity may step into alignment with cosmic order.

By acknowledging Magha's superiority, the tradition encourages humanity to attune itself more acutely to the essence of time—to distinguish when it necessitates exertion and when it bestows grace.

3. Snāna, dāna, tapas, and pitṛ-kārya

Snāna, dāna, tapas, and *pitṛ-kārya* together form the sacred quadrilateral of dharmic living, especially illuminated during auspicious periods like *Magha Māsa*. These are not isolated rituals but integrated pathways through which the individual harmonizes body, society, cosmos, and lineage. *Snāna* purifies the inner and outer self by aligning the body with cosmic memory; *dāna* restores moral balance through selfless giving; *tapas* refine consciousness through disciplined restraint; and *pitṛ-kārya* heals the invisible continuum between past, present, and future generations. Practiced together, they transform time-bound existence into a sacred journey, where personal effort becomes a bridge to ancestral grace and cosmic order.

1. Snāna: Immersion into Cosmic Memory:

Magha Snāna is the heart of this sacred month. Scriptures insist that bathing at dawn in rivers, lakes, or even mentally consecrated waters during Magha purifies sins of body, speech, and mind.

This is not hygiene—it is re-entry into cosmic memory. Water, having witnessed creation, is believed to carry primordial intelligence. When one enters it during Magha, personal time dissolves into cosmic time. The chill of the water disciplines the body; the stillness of dawn disciplines the mind.

The *Padma Purāṇa* declares that a single *Magha Snāna* equals years of penance. Even those unable to travel to *tīrthas* are instructed to invoke sacred rivers through mantra, affirming that intention sanctifies space.

Mantra for Invoking Sacred Rivers (Tīrtha-Āvāhana Mantra)

गङ्गे च यमुने चैव

गोदावरि सरस्वति ।

नर्मदे सिन्धु कावेरी

जलेऽस्मिन् सन्निधिं कुरु ॥

Gaṅge ca Yamune caiva
Godāvari Sarasvatī |
Narmade Sindhu Kāverī

jale'smin sannidhiṁ kuru ||

"O sacred Gaṅgā, Yamunā, Godāvarī, Sarasvatī, Narmadā, Sindhu, and Kāverī—
Please be present in this water and sanctify it with your divine presence."

Spiritual Significance:

This ancient mantra affirms a central dharmic truth: intention sanctifies space. For those unable to travel to distant *tīrthas*, the sacred rivers are invoked through remembrance and sound. By chanting this mantra with devotion, ordinary water is transformed into *tīrtha*, allowing the practitioner to participate in the same sacred time and grace as a pilgrim at the riverbanks. Here, geography yields to consciousness, and faith bridges all distances.

2. Dāna: Restoring the Flow of Dharma:

Charity (*Dāna*) during *Magha Māsa* is not viewed as personal generosity or moral virtue alone; it is understood as cosmic restitution. The *Purāṇic* vision teaches that the universe is sustained by balance—between taking and giving, accumulation and release. Possession and hoarding disrupt this balance in human life. *Dāna*, especially during Magha, is the conscious act of returning what was never truly ours back to the cosmic flow.

The gifts prescribed—food, clothing, ghee, gold, knowledge, and shelter—are not chosen at random. Each represents a fundamental support of life. Offering them during Magha is equivalent to strengthening the very pillars upon which society and *dharma* stand. Such giving is said to please not only the recipient but also the unseen forces that uphold order, for it heals the subtle fractures caused by greed and neglect.

Magha infuses *dāna* with a rare spiritual potency. In this sacred month, giving dissolves the fear of loss and restores the consciousness of abundance. The giver realizes that life is not sustained by what is held but by what flows. The scriptures therefore affirm that what is offered in Magha returns multiplied—not necessarily as material wealth, but as clarity of mind, unseen protection, emotional resilience, and inner strength. These are forms of wealth that cannot be stolen or exhausted.

More importantly, *dāna* prevents spirituality from turning inward and self-contained. Devotion that does not express itself through compassion risks becoming sterile. Through dāna, inner awakening finds outward expression, transforming personal piety into social harmony. Hunger is eased, dignity is restored, and bonds between human beings are renewed.

Thus, *dāna* in Magha becomes an act of participation in cosmic order—where the heart opens, hands extend, and the universe quietly restores itself through the simple grace of giving.

3. Tapas: Austerity as Inner Churning:

Tapas, in its deepest sense, does not signify punishment of the body but the generation of inner heat that transforms consciousness. During *Magha Māsa*, tapas is prescribed not as a rigid discipline, but as a measured practice aligned with one's capacity. The scriptures recognize human diversity and therefore allow multiple forms of tapas—fasting or moderated eating, periods of silence (*mauna*), celibacy (*brahmacarya*), night vigils, regulated sleep, *japa*, and disciplined prayer. What sanctifies tapas is not its severity, but its sincerity and continuity.

The true purpose of Magha tapas is inner Samudra Manthana —the churning of one's own inner ocean. Just as the cosmic ocean was churned to bring forth hidden treasures, austerity churns the subconscious layers of the mind. When habitual comforts are withdrawn, the body resists and the mind react. This resistance is not a failure; it is the beginning of purification. In the heat of restraint, dormant impressions (*saṁskāras*), unresolved desires, fears, and memories rise to the surface.

As the body learns discipline, the mind sheds its inertia (*tamas*). Restlessness gives way to clarity, and indulgence is replaced by attentiveness. The *Purāṇas* explain that certain *karmas* are subtle, deeply embedded across lifetimes, and cannot be neutralized through ordinary virtuous acts alone. These karmic residues dissolve only when conscious restraint is combined with sacred time. Magha provides this rare conjunction. *Tapas* performed in this month is said to burn karmic seeds before they sprout into future experience.

Importantly, *Magha tapas* are not oriented toward self-negation but self-refinement. It does not aim to weaken life but to purify its direction. The temporary discomfort of austerity produces a lasting lightness of being. What is renounced is not joy, but excess, not life, but bondage.

In this process, austerity becomes alchemy. Just as base metals are transmuted into gold through fire, ordinary consciousness is transformed into clarity through tapas. The practitioner emerges not diminished, but expanded—freer, quieter, and more aligned with inner truth. In *Magha Māsa,* this alchemy unfolds with gentleness, as time itself supports the seeker's inner churning.

4. Pitṛ-Kārya: Healing the Ancestral Continuum:

In the dharmic vision of existence, life does not begin with birth nor end with death. It flows as an unbroken ancestral continuum, where the living, the departed, and the unborn are bound together through subtle threads of *karma*, memory, and obligation. *Pitṛ-kārya,* the sacred duty toward ancestors, arises from this understanding. Among all times prescribed for ancestral rites, *Magha Māsa* is regarded as uniquely potent, for during this month the distance between worlds grows thin and permeable.

The *Smṛtis* and *Purāṇas* describe *Magha* as a period when the *pitṛ-loka* draws closer to the human realm. Just as certain seasons allow seeds to germinate with ease, Magha allows ancestral energies to receive offerings and blessings without obstruction. Rituals such as *śrāddha, tarpana,* and silent remembrance performed during this month are said to reach ancestors directly, carrying nourishment, peace, and release.

Pitṛ-kārya is not merely an act of gratitude toward forebears; it is a process of karmic reconciliation. The tradition recognizes that unresolved desires, unfulfilled duties, and unfinished emotional bonds do not vanish with death. They continue to echo through generations, subtly shaping circumstances, tendencies, and inner conflicts. When offerings are made during Magha, these lingering impressions are soothed, and the ancestral stream is gradually purified.

The *Smṛtis* teach that honouring ancestors restores lineage harmony. A lineage is not only biological; it is spiritual and psychological. When *pitṛ-kārya* is neglected, descendants may unknowingly carry invisible burdens—recurring obstacles, emotional unrest, or a sense of incompleteness. Magha rituals act as a gentle release, allowing both ancestors and descendants to move forward unencumbered.

Significantly, *pitṛ-kārya* during *Magha* is said to benefit not only those who have departed but also future generations. By mending the past, the practitioner paves the way for future generations. Thus, Magha becomes a bridge across time—linking memory with possibility, obligation with blessing.

In this way, *Magha Māsa* transforms ancestral duty into a

profound act of compassion. Personal liberation expands into intergenerational healing, reminding the seeker that no one walks alone. Each step taken in awareness lifts not just the self, but the entire lineage—past, present, and future—into greater harmony with dharma.

4. Magha Māsa: When Heaven Touches Human Time

Magha Māsa reveals a profound and compassionate truth of the dharmic worldview: liberation is not remote, abstract, or reserved for a distant afterlife. It is woven into the rhythm of time itself. The sacred does not wait at the end of existence; it returns cyclically, season after season, offering renewal to those who are attentive. *Magha* arrives each year not as an obligation, but as an invitation—quiet, patient, and merciful—asking only awareness, humility, and willingness.

Unlike paths that demand radical withdrawal from life, *Magha* meets a human being where one already stands. It recognizes limitations, exhaustion, and imperfections, yet still creates a pathway to grace. In this month, time softens. The natural world becomes articulate: rivers are no longer streams of water but carriers of memory and mercy; dawns are no longer routine but thresholds of transformation. To bathe, to give, to restrain oneself, or to remember one's ancestors during Magha is to enter a living conversation with the cosmos.

The tradition poetically affirms that in Magha, rivers speak, ancestors listen, and the gods draw near. These are not metaphors alone. Rivers, infused with sacred time, absorb human intention and return it as purification. Ancestors, released from distance, receive remembrance as nourishment and respond with unseen blessings. The gods, representing cosmic order and intelligence, are said to incline toward human effort, witnessing even the smallest act of sincerity.

To live *Magha* is to recognize that time itself can be a carrier of grace. Not all moments are equal; some are laden with possibility. When such time is honoured—through discipline, generosity, and remembrance—it descends into life as quiet transformation. Burdens lighten, clarity emerges, and life realigns without force.

Magha Māsa thus stands as a recurring assurance that the divine has not withdrawn from the world. Heaven continues to touch human time—gently, cyclically, and faithfully—reminding humanity that liberation is not somewhere else. It is here, now, when time itself becomes sacred.

CHAPTER 6: MAHA MAGHA—ALIGNMENT OF TIME, SPACE, AND CONSCIOUSNESS

Maha Magha is not merely an intensified version of *Magha Māsa*, nor is it interchangeable with *Kumbha*. It represents a rare convergence where time (*kāla*), space (*deśa*), and consciousness (*cetanā*) align in perfect resonance. When this triad comes into harmony, sacred time ceases to be symbolic and becomes experiential. Maha Magha is that threshold—when the cosmic order momentarily reveals itself in human time.

1. Magha vs. Maha Magha vs. Kumbha: Distinctions in Sacred Time

Magha Māsa occurs annually. It is a recurring season of purification, discipline, and remembrance, accessible to all. It sanctifies time, offering a yearly opportunity for spiritual renewal through *snāna, dāna, tapas,* and *pitṛ-kārya.*

Maha Magha, however, is exceptional. It arises when *Magha Māsa* coincides with powerful celestial alignments, particularly at highly charged *tīrthas*—most notably *Prayāga*, the confluence of *Gaṅgā, Yamunā,* and the invisible *Sarasvatī*. Here, sacred time is not only present; it is concentrated. What is spread across the month of Magha becomes distilled into specific days and moments.

Kumbha operates on an even larger scale. It is governed by Jupiter's twelve-year cycle and complex planetary configurations. Kumbha sanctifies space—specific locations become cosmically activated. *Maha Magha*, by contrast, sanctifies time within space. When Kumbha occurs during *Magha*, *Maha Magha* emerges as their intersection—the peak moment of sanctity, where both time and place reach maximum spiritual potency.

Thus:

1. *Magha* purifies time annually.
2. *Kumbha* consecrates space cyclically.
3. *Maha Magha* aligns both into a single, luminous threshold.

2. Jyotiṣa and Metaphysical Convergence

Jyotiṣa is not fortune-telling; it is the science of cosmic rhythm. According to *Jyotiṣa*, certain planetary configurations generate fields of heightened consciousness. During *Maha Magha*, the Sun's position, the Moon's *Nakṣatra*, Jupiter's influence, and the gravitational harmony of celestial bodies converge to recreate a primordial cosmic condition.

This convergence affects not only the heavens but also human psychology and subtle physiology. The mind becomes naturally contemplative, emotions soften, and the sense of individuality loosens. This is why ancient seers prescribed collective rituals, pilgrimages, and mass bathing during such periods. The environment itself supports transcendence.

Metaphysically, *Maha Magha* represents a moment when cosmic memory reactivates. Just as iron filings align effortlessly in a magnetic field, human consciousness aligns with dharma when exposed to these cosmic currents. Liberation becomes less a matter of striving and more a matter of surrendering to alignment.

3. Maha Magha as a Doorway to Liberation

Liberation is often imagined as the culmination of lifetimes of effort. *Maha Magha* offers a different insight: liberation is also situational. When time, space, and intention align, the weight of karma momentarily lightens. The self-glimpses freedom not through escape, but through resonance.

Bathing during *Maha Magha* is therefore not symbolic purification—it is participation in cosmic reset. Charity becomes karmic release. Austerity becomes effortless clarity. Remembrance of ancestors dissolves inherited burdens. Even silent presence at the *tīrtha* is considered transformative.

The scriptures affirm that acts performed during *Maha Magha* yield results ordinarily attained only through severe tapas. This does not diminish effort; it reveals grace as an equal force. Maha Magha is grace made visible in time.

Ultimately, Maha Magha teaches that liberation is not opposed to life. It emerges when life is lived in harmony with cosmic intelligence. Maha Magha is that doorway—open briefly, rhythmically, compassionately—through which humanity is invited to step into freedom. When time aligns, space awakens, and consciousness bows, the path opens by itself.

PART III

SACRED GEOGRAPHY OF THE SOUTH Where Land Remembers

CHAPTER 7: BHARATHAPUZHA —THE RIVER THAT SHAPED KERALA'S SOUL

Sacred Geography of South India

The sacred geography of South India is not merely mapped in temples and rivers but etched into the memory of the land itself. Here, mountains, forests, and waterways are living witnesses to tapas, revelation, and timeless devotion. Every shrine marks a point where consciousness once awakened, and the land continues to remember that encounter. This geography is not static space but experienced time, where myth, history, and inner realization converge. To walk this land is to enter a dialogue with memory—one where earth becomes scripture and place itself guides the seeker toward remembrance and renewal.

Bharathapuzha

Among the rivers of the Indian subcontinent, *Bharathapuzha*, lovingly known as *Nila*, flows through a realm far deeper than geography. She is not merely a river coursing through Kerala; she is a living current of memory, devotion, and civilization. Along her banks, Kerala learned not only how to cultivate land but also how to pray, sing, reflect, and dream. *Bharathapuzha* did more than nourish soil—she shaped the inner landscape of a people.

To describe *Bharathapuzha* as a river is a cartographic necessity; to the people of Kerala, she is *Nila*—a mother who nurtured generations, a muse who inspired poets and musicians, and a silent witness to centuries of spiritual striving. Revered as *Dakshina Ganga*, the Ganga of the South, she is the sacred thread that weaves together Kerala's spiritual inheritance and cultural continuity. Through her gentle flow, the sacred and the everyday have long met without division.

The Geographical Journey

Bharathapuzha rises in the Anaimalai Hills of the Western Ghats, at an elevation of nearly 1,964 meters, where mist, forest, and silence converge. From this high cradle, she journeys *209 kilometers* westward before surrendering her waters to the Arabian Sea at *Ponnani*. Unlike many of Kerala's rivers that rush impetuously toward the ocean, Nila moves with a measured, contemplative grace, lingering as though unwilling to abandon the land she sustains.

Her path winds through the heart of Kerala, touching the districts of Palakkad, Thrissur, and Malappuram, carrying with her the rhythms of agrarian life, temple bells, and ancestral memory.

Her strength is gathered from four principal tributaries—*Kalpathipuzha, Gayathripuzha, Thuthapuzha,* and *Kannadipuzha* —each contributing its character to her flow. Together, they form a river system that has quietly sustained one of the most culturally fertile regions of South India.

Flowing through the *Palakkad Gap*, a unique break in the Western Ghats, *Bharathapuzha* becomes the primary freshwater source for this rain-shadow region. In doing so, she earns her place as the lifeline of Kerala's celebrated "Rice Bowl." Here, her waters do not merely irrigate fields; they uphold livelihoods, rituals, and a way of life shaped by patience and reverence.

Thus, *Bharathapuzha* stands as more than a river's course from mountain to sea. She is a journey of civilization itself—from source to surrender, from memory to meaning, from land to soul.

1. Mythological Origins of Nila: A River Born of Austerity

The origins of *Bharathapuzha* are wrapped in sacred myth, where rivers arise not from glaciers alone but from tapas and divine intention. Tradition associates Nila with the blessings of Lord Shiva, whose presence sanctifies the Western Ghats. Some legends speak of sage *Agastya*, the great southern seer, whose penance caused sacred waters to descend and flow toward the western sea, balancing the spiritual energies of the land.

In *Purāṇic* imagination, *Bharathapuzha* is described as a river of inner coolness and restraint, mirroring the qualities of ascetic wisdom. Unlike torrential rivers of conquest, *Nila* flows with quiet dignity, teaching that endurance, not force, sustains civilization. Its waters are believed to carry the blessings of ancient *yāgas* and hermitages that once lined its banks, making every ripple a continuation of prayer.

Thus, *Nila* is not only a natural phenomenon but also a manifestation of spiritual resolve, a river born where sages conversed with the cosmos.

2. The River in Kerala's Spiritual, Literary, and Cultural Memory

If Kerala has a collective memory, *Bharathapuzha* is its flood stream. The river flows through the heart of the state, touching temples, villages, and minds alike. It has been the silent witness to Vedic recitations, temple festivals, and household rites, serving as the ritual axis of everyday life.

Spiritually, *Bharathapuzha* has been central to temple traditions and sacred observances such as *Magha Snāna* and ancestral rites. Its banks hosted scholars, yogis, and musicians who saw the river not as scenery but as a living presence.

Nila is the only river that has inspired Kerala's writers. Poets and authors have evoked *Bharathapuzha* as mother, witness, and lament—especially in times of cultural loss and ecological neglect. In Malayalam literature, the river often appears as a symbol of continuity amid change, a reminder of a quieter, more rooted past.

Bharathapuzha helped Kerala's classical arts grow. Kathakali, Koodiyattam, and Carnatic music flourished in the riverine settlements along its banks. Families of artists, scholars, and priests drew sustenance—material and spiritual—from its waters. The river thus became an unwritten university, transmitting culture not through institutions, but through lived tradition.

3. Bharathapuzha as Dakshina Ganga: The Southern Flow of Liberation

Bharathapuzha is revered as *Dakshina Ganga*—the Ganga of the South. This title is not honorary; it reflects lived spiritual practice. Just as the Ganga in the north is associated with liberation and ancestral release, Bharathapuzha has long served as a sacred site for *śrāddha*, *tarpana*, and final rites.

For countless families, the river has been the chosen place to offer farewell to ancestors, believing that *Nila* carries prayers gently toward the cosmic ocean. The belief that liberation flows southward through Bharathapuzha speaks to a deeper truth:

grace adapts to geography. What the Ganga offers in the north, Bharathapuzha offers in the south—with the same sanctity, though expressed in a quieter cadence.

As Dakshina Ganga, Bharathapuzha unites time, lineage, and land. It is where past generations are remembered, present lives are consecrated, and future blessings are invoked. Even in its present fragility, the river continues to whisper its ancient promise—that liberation does not roar; it flows.

The River That Remembers

Bharathapuzha is not only Kerala's river—it is Kerala's conscience. To remember *Nila* is to remember a way of life rooted in restraint, reverence, and rhythm with nature. As long as the river flows—even faintly—the soul of Kerala continues to breathe.

In listening to Bharathapuzha, one listens to the land remembering itself.

CHAPTER 8: TRIMŪRTI SAṄGAMAM AND THE RIVER TĪRTHAS

In the sacred imagination of Bhārata, rivers are not mere flows of water—they are corridors of consciousness, carrying memory, merit, and liberation. Along the banks of *Bharathapuzha (Nila)*, this truth finds one of its most profound expressions in what tradition reveres as *Trimūrti Saṅgamam*—the subtle convergence of *Brahmā, Viṣṇu,* and *Śiva* within sacred geography. Here, land, water, and worship merge into a living *tīrtha*, where time bends gently toward eternity.

1. Thirunavaya, Thavanur, and Sacred Alignments

Along the sacred course of *Bharathapuzha*, certain spaces do not merely lie beside the river—they stand revealed by it. Among these, *Thirunavaya* and *Thavanur* emerge as luminous centers where geography, ritual, and cosmic principle converge. They are not isolated holy sites but anchors of a larger sacred geometry, through which the river itself becomes a bearer of divine order.

1. Thirunavaya: Where Preservation Becomes Order:

Thirunavaya has long been revered as a *Vaiṣṇava kṣetra*, a place where *Viṣṇu* as the preserver (*sthiti*) manifests not only in icon and temple but also in the rhythm of social and cosmic life.

Tradition remembers Thirunavaya as the ground where dharma was ritually renewed—through yajñas, assemblies of scholars, and royal consecrations. Kings did not merely rule from here; they were consecrated into responsibility, reminded that power derives legitimacy only when aligned with cosmic order.

The famed *Mamankam* assemblies, held on these banks, were not merely political gatherings but ritual affirmations of continuity—that kingdoms may rise and fall, but dharma must endure. In this sense, *Thirunavaya* represents *Viṣṇu* not as a distant divinity, but as a living regulation of time, duty, and harmony. Here, preservation descends from the heavens and takes shape as law, custom, and collective memory.

2. Thavanur: The Realm of Renunciation and Inner Fire:

If *Thirunavaya* speaks of order and continuity, *Thavanur* answers in a different register—that of *Śiva*, the great renouncer. Associated with silence, austerity, and inward intensity, *Thavanur* is remembered as a *tapas-bhūmi*, where seekers withdrew from the noise of the world to confront its essence.

Śiva's presence here is not expressed through grandeur, but through stillness and restraint. The very name *Thavanur* echoes *tapas*—the inner heat that burns ignorance and reveals truth. Forest hermitages, meditation grounds, and ascetic lineages once flourished here, forming a counter current to the ceremonial life of *Thirunavaya*. Where one affirmed worldly order, the other questioned attachment to it.

Together, they establish a sacred polarity: *pravṛtti* and *nivṛtti*, engagement and withdrawal, governance and renunciation—both essential for civilizational balance.

3. Bharathapuzha as the Unseen Brahmā:

Flowing silently between these two sacred poles is

Bharathapuzha, assuming the subtle role of *Brahmā*, the creative principle. Unlike *Viṣṇu* and *Śiva, Brahmā* is rarely worshipped in temple form; his presence is diffuse, continuous, and sustaining. So too is the river—unceasingly generating life, culture, and memory.

The river binds the opposites. It nourishes ritual at *Thirunavaya* and solitude at *Thavanur* alike. It carries the ashes of renunciation and the waters of consecration in the same flow. In this triadic vision, *Bharathapuzha* is not merely water—it is creation in motion, the silent ground upon which preservation and dissolution enact their roles.

Thus, the river itself becomes *Trimūrti Sañcāra*—the *Trimūrti* in movement.

4. A Living Mandala of Sacred Geography:

Such an alignment, tradition insists, is never accidental. *Purāṇic* cosmology teaches that certain lands awaken when cosmic currents (*ṛta-dhārās*) intersect. These currents invite divine principles to root themselves in earth, water, and human action. *Thirunavaya* and *Thavanur* stand as markers of such intersections—nodes in a living mandala inscribed not on stone, but across landscape and time.

Pilgrims who walk these riverbanks participate in this mandala, whether consciously or not. Each step becomes a circumambulation, each immersion, a rite of passage through creation, preservation, and dissolution. The land teaches without speech, and the river initiates without doctrine. Here, sacred alignment is not something to be observed—it is something to be entered, inhabited, and remembered.

2. Temples, Āśramas, and Forgotten Tapas Grounds

Layers of Sacred Memory Along Bharathapuzha

1. Temples as Living Nodes of Ritual Civilization:

Along the banks of *Bharathapuzha*, temples rise not merely as places of worship but as repositories of lived *dharma*. Many of these shrines, modest today in scale and ornamentation, were once the centres of expansive ritual ecosystems. Daily *pūjā*, seasonal *yajñas*, river-based *saṁskāras*, and communal observances unfolded here in rhythmic harmony with the flow of the river.

These temples functioned as interfaces between cosmic order and social life. Festivals marked celestial movements; rituals synchronized human activity with lunar and solar cycles. The temple bell did more than call devotees—it regulated time itself. Even now, beneath weathered stone and quiet corridors, these spaces carry an accumulated sanctity, built layer by layer through centuries of devotion.

2. Āśramas: Cradles of Tapas and Transmission:

Interwoven with the temples were *āśramas*, often situated slightly away from the village centre, closer to forest edges or secluded river bends. These were not institutions in the modern sense but living lineages of discipline. Here, sages and teachers practiced prolonged *tapas*, cultivating inner fire through austerity, restraint, and contemplative absorption.

Knowledge in these āśramas was not written but embodied and transmitted orally—through dialogue, silence, observation, and daily practice. Students did not merely study dharma; they lived it, absorbing values through service, simplicity, and sustained proximity to the teacher. *Bharathapuzha*, flowing nearby, became both witness and participant—providing water for rituals and a constant reminder of impermanence and continuity.

These āśramas shaped generations of scholars, healers, ritual specialists, and householders, ensuring that wisdom did not remain abstract but flowed into social life.

3. Forgotten Tapas Grounds: Where Silence Still Speaks:

With the passage of time, many tapas grounds—sites of intense meditation and ascetic practice—have slipped beyond formal memory. No inscriptions mark them; no festivals announce their presence. They survive in local lore, place names, and half-whispered legends passed down through families.

Yet, within the dharmic imagination, such places are never truly abandoned. It is believed that *tapas* leave an imprint upon the land itself. Even when huts collapse and names fade, the subtle charge (*śakti*) remains. The air feels different, the silence heavier, and the mind naturally inclined toward stillness.

Pilgrims and villagers often speak of an unspoken reverence—of pausing instinctively, lowering one's voice, or feeling drawn inward at certain river bends. Here, silence becomes the teacher, conveying what words no longer can.

4. Sacred Geography Beyond Monumentality:

These forgotten centres remind us that Kerala's spiritual heritage was never confined to grand temples alone. Monumental architecture was only one expression of sanctity. Equally sacred were forest clearings, river confluences, shaded groves, and humble hermitages where seekers pursued liberation amidst ordinary life.

In these spaces, life and *mokṣa* coexisted without contradiction. Agriculture, family, ritual, and renunciation flowed together, mirroring the river's own course. Spirituality here was not an escape from the world but a deep atonement to it.

5. Bharathapuzha as Keeper of Invisible Lineages:

Through all these layers—temples, *āśramas*, and vanished tapas grounds—*Bharathapuzha* remains the silent custodian. She carries not only water but also memory, preserving invisible lineages that shaped Kerala's soul. Her banks teach that what truly endures is not stone or structure, but intent, discipline, and lived wisdom.

To walk along her course is to move through strata of sacred time, where every quiet stretch may once have echoed with mantra, and every bend may still shelter the residue of realization.

3. River-Based Rituals as Kerala's Dharmic Ecology

Where Spiritual Practice and Natural Order Become One

1. Dharma in Communion with Nature, Not Mastery Over It:

Kerala's dharmic vision did not arise from an urge to conquer nature but from a reverential intimacy with it. Rivers were not treated as inert resources to be exploited but as living presences—mothers, witnesses, and moral regulators. In this worldview, *dharma* unfolded in dialogue with earth, water, wind, and season, not in isolation from them.

River-based rituals formed the backbone of this ecological spirituality. They ensured that human conduct remained aligned with cosmic and environmental rhythms, preventing excess, arrogance, and alienation. *Bharathapuzha*, flowing through the heart of Kerala, became a moral and spiritual axis, shaping how communities lived, worshipped, and remembered.

2. Snāna: Purification Through Elemental Participation:

Daily and seasonal *snāna* (ritual bathing) was not merely an act of bodily cleansing but a conscious surrender to the elemental order. Entering the river at dawn, when the world is hushed and light is nascent, trained the mind in humility and attentiveness.

Cold water awakened discipline; flowing currents reminded the bather of impermanence. Through *snāna*, the individual did not stand apart from nature but participated in it, allowing the river to wash not only the body but also accumulated mental residues. Thus, personal purification became an ecological act—one that respected water as sacred and finite.

3. Tarpana and Śrāddha: Ancestral Memory as Ecological Continuity:

Tarpana and *śrāddha*, performed on riverbanks, linked the living, the departed, and the landscape into a single continuum. Ancestors were not imagined as distant spirits but as participants in the ongoing life of the land. Offerings made to them through river water affirmed that lineage, memory, and ecology are inseparable.

Seasonal timing of these rites ensured that ancestral remembrance coincided with natural transitions—monsoons, harvest cycles, and solar movements. In honouring the past, communities learned responsibility toward the future, cultivating a sense that to damage the river was to disrupt ancestral peace itself.

4. Utsavas and Collective Rituals: Ecology as Social Harmony:

Festivals and *utsavas* centered around the river transformed ecology into collective celebration. Processions, river offerings, communal baths, and temple rituals brought entire villages to the water's edge, dissolving social boundaries in shared reverence.

These gatherings regulated social life, preventing

fragmentation. The river became a neutral and unifying space, where caste, profession, and status softened before a greater sacred order. Through repetition across generations, the river taught society how to gather without greed, celebrate without excess, and rejoice without rupture.

5. Time, Season, and Austerity: Climate as Spiritual Instructor:

Austerities and vows were traditionally chosen in accordance with climatic and seasonal patterns. Certain fasts coincided with cooler months; intense tapas avoided periods of ecological stress. This sensitivity ensured that spirituality did not become self-violent or environmentally negligent.

By synchronizing discipline with climate, *Bharathapuzha* instructed practitioners in restraint and adaptability. Dharma was thus not rigid law but responsive intelligence, capable of adjusting to nature's signals.

6. The River as Guru: Teaching Balance and Renewal:

Through all these practices, *Bharathapuzha* emerged not merely as a site of ritual but as a guru in flowing form. Her cycles of abundance and scarcity taught moderation. Her patience taught endurance. Her silence taught introspection.

This dharmic ecology ensured that spirituality remained embodied and experiential, not abstract theology. It was felt in the shock of cold water at dawn, heard in temple bells carried across ripples, and seen in generations gathering instinctively at the riverbank.

7. A Model of Sacred Sustainability:

Kerala's river-based rituals reveal a civilizational insight now urgently relevant: when nature is treated as sacred, sustainability arises organically. Ecology is preserved not by regulation alone, but by reverence.

In this way, *Bharathapuzha* sustained more than crops and settlements. She sustained a way of being where spiritual awakening, social harmony, and environmental care flowed together—like the river herself, steady, patient, and life-giving.

A Confluence Beyond Water

Trimūrti Saṅgamam along *Bharathapuzha* reveals a deeper truth: when sacred geography is honoured, divinity becomes inhabitable. Rivers remember, land responds, and human consciousness awakens in resonance.

In these tīrthas, Kerala's soul learned that liberation does not always require ascent to distant heavens. Sometimes, it waits quietly where a river flows, where the *Trimūrti* converge, and where time itself pauses to listen.

PART IV

THE FORGOTTEN SOUTHERN MAHA MAGHA Silence Without Erasure

CHAPTER 9: SOUTHERN TRADITIONS OF KUMBH AND MAGHA SNĀNA

Where Sacred Time Flowed Without Proclamation

While the northern plains echo with the thunder of Kumbha gatherings, the South remembers Maha Magha differently—quietly, inwardly, without spectacle. Here, sacred time was not announced by crowds but absorbed into rivers, villages, and daily rites. Though largely absent from popular memory, Southern Maha Magha was never erased. It survives in silent *snānas*, ancestral offerings, and temple rhythms that continue without proclamation. This chapter listens to that silence—not as loss, but as a subtler continuity, where sacred time flows unseen, awaiting remembrance rather than revival.

1. Evidence from South Indian Texts: The Quiet Witness of Scripture

Continuity Without Spectacle

The spiritual genius of the South India reveals itself not through proclamation, but through unbroken practice. Its authority rests in continuity—rituals repeated faithfully across centuries, even when unrecorded by grand narratives. While the northern plains came to be identified with vast congregational Kumbhas that captured popular and political imagination, South Indian textual traditions preserved Magha *Snāna* in a subtler, inward register, equally potent yet deliberately understated.

1. Purāṇic Universality: Sanctity Beyond Geography:

The *Skanda, Padma,* and *Brahmāṇḍa Purāṇas,* revered throughout Bhārata, articulate a crucial principle often overlooked: the sanctity of Magha is temporal and moral, not territorial. These texts repeatedly affirm that tīrthas arise wherever rivers flow with *śraddhā* and where human conduct aligns with dharma. The descent of sacred time is thus conditional not upon location, but upon inner and collective preparedness.

This universal vision made it unnecessary for the South to replicate northern models of mass pilgrimage. Rivers of the South—though absent from imperial chronicles—were fully capable of receiving *Maha Magha* through right observance. Scripture itself legitimized this decentralized sanctity.

2. Sthala-Purāṇas and Temple Māhātmyas: Localized Eternity:

South Indian *sthala-purāṇas* and temple māhātmyas offer a different kind of testimony. They rarely narrate spectacular assemblies; instead, they record seasonal disciplines—*Magha snāna* at dawn, *tarpana* on riverbanks, prescribed *dānas*, and heightened *vrata* observances. These texts situate Magha firmly within local geographies, sanctifying village rivers, temple tanks, and confluences.

Such literature does not shout. It documents lived rhythm—the kind of sacred order that does not require historical interruption to prove its legitimacy. In this way, local texts preserve eternity on small scales, ensuring that cosmic time enters daily life without fanfare.

3. Āgamic Literature: Discipline Over Display:

Āgamic commentaries from the South further reinforce this temperament. Their concern is not crowds or calendars of spectacle, but precision of practice—the correct hour of *snāna*, the purity of intention, and the alignment of *mantra*, *mudrā*, and mental focus. Magha, in these texts, is a disciplinary intensifier, not a festival of numbers.

This reflects a philosophical orientation deeply influenced by *Advaita* and *tapas*. Liberation was pursued through inward clarity rather than outward movement. Sacred time was absorbed through discipline, not approached through pilgrimage alone.

4. Magha as a Season, Not an Event:

In Kerala, *Tamilakam*, and the *Deccan*, *Magha* emerges not as a singular event to be attended, but as a season to be inhabited. Households adjusted daily routines; temples modified ritual intensity; rivers received offerings with quiet regularity. This seasonal sanctity allowed Magha to permeate life rather than interrupt it.

The absence of textual emphasis on mass gatherings is therefore not omission but intentional cultural choice. It reflects a civilization that valued depth over display, absorption over announcement, and inwardness over visibility.

5. Silence as Scriptural Testimony:

In the South, silence itself becomes a form of evidence. The lack of spectacular description signals confidence—a knowing that sacred time does not require validation through scale. Scripture here acts not as advertisement, but as a quiet witness, trusting that those attuned will recognize Magha when it arrives.

Thus, South Indian texts do not deny *Maha Magha*. They host it differently—within continuity, restraint, and lived dharma—proving that what is sacred need not be loud to be eternal.

2. Kerala's Unique Ritual Grammar: Subtlety as Sacred Intelligence

Kerala developed a distinct ritual grammar, shaped by its ecology, climate, and cultural ethos. Abundant rivers, monsoons, and closely knit village life made daily sacredness more central than episodic pilgrimage. Here, Magha *snāna* unfolded in village *tīrthas*, temple tanks, and rivers like *Bharathapuzha*—not as a mass convergence, but as a distributed sanctity.

Rituals were woven seamlessly into domestic and communal life. Early-morning river *snāna,* baths, quiet *śrāddhas*, temple lamps lit before sun rise and restrained fasting marked Magha. The emphasis was not on gathering multitudes but on precision, purity, and inwardness.

This grammar reflects a philosophical orientation rooted in *Advaita* and *tapas*. Liberation was understood as inward alignment, not outward movement. Thus, Kerala preserved Magha as a discipline of consciousness, not a spectacle of numbers.

3. Essence Preserved, Scale Forgotten: The Survival of Sacred Meaning

Over time, historical shifts—political change, colonial disruption, and modern amnesia—obscured the scale of southern Magha observances. Large assemblies faded, pilgrimage routes fell silent, and rivers lost their ritual centrality. Yet, the essence endured.

The core principles of *Maha Magha*—purification through water, alignment with cosmic time, ancestral healing, and ethical restraint—continued quietly in households and temples. What was forgotten was not meaning, but memory of magnitude.

This forgetting itself reflects a deeper truth: sacred time does not depend on crowds to remain potent. A single devotee entering the river at dawn with awareness embodies the same cosmic alignment as thousands gathered elsewhere.

4. Silence as Preservation, Not Loss

The Southern tradition teaches that silence can be a form of safeguarding. By refusing spectacle, it protected rituals from erosion into performance. What survived was not diluted by excess but distilled through restraint.

Thus, the Southern Maha Magha stands as a counter-memory to modern assumptions—that visibility equals vitality. Here, absence of noise is not absence of life, but a sign of spiritual maturity.

5. Remembering Without Revivalism

To rediscover Southern Magha is not to recreate northern *Kumbhas* in the South, but to relearn an older rhythm—where sacred time descends softly, rivers receive devotion without announcement, and liberation remains accessible without travel.

This chapter does not call for revival through imitation but for recognition through remembrance. The waters are still flowing. The season still arrives. What is needed is not reconstruction, but re-attunement. In this quiet remembering, Southern *Maha*

Magha continues—not as history, but as a living possibility.

CHAPTER 10: WHY MAHA MAGHA FELL SILENT

When Sacred Time Withdrew from the Public Eye

1. Colonial Rupture and Ritual Fragmentation: The Breaking of Sacred Continuity

Maha Magha did not disappear in the South—it was dispersed. The first deep fracture came with colonial rule, which did not merely occupy territory but reordered time itself. Indigenous calendars, ritual cycles, and river-based observances were pushed to the margins, replaced by administrative time, industrial rhythms, and secular public space.

Colonial governance viewed rivers as resources to be measured, not sanctities to be approached. Sacred geography was mapped, taxed, dammed, and redirected. Temple endowments were weakened, *āśramas* lost patronage, and ritual specialists were reduced to relics of a "past civilization." Without institutional support, large-scale congregational observances dissolved into household rites.

Ritual did not die—but it fragmented. What was once collective memory became private survival.

2. Loss of Civilizational Confidence: When Silence Became Shame

Equally damaging was the internalization of colonial judgment. Over time, ritual practices came to be seen by the colonized themselves as irrational, unscientific, or embarrassing. A civilization that once trusted its own cosmology began to doubt its relevance.

Maha Magha, rooted in metaphysical understandings of time, water, and consciousness, could not easily defend itself in the language of colonial rationalism. Without confidence, communities stopped explaining—and eventually stopped gathering. Silence, once a sign of inward depth, turned into withdrawal. This was not forgetting through ignorance but forgetting through hesitation—a reluctance to stand publicly in one's own sacred logic.

3. Ritual Without Congregation vs. Congregation Without Memory

The modern period introduced a paradox. In the South, *Magha* rituals survived without congregation—performed faithfully by individuals and families yet disconnected from collective affirmation. In contrast, elsewhere, congregations expanded even as memory thinned, with participation often detached from understanding.

Ritual without congregation preserves depth but lacks visibility. Congregation without memory preserves scale but risks emptiness. The Southern Maha Magha chose the former, valuing continuity of meaning over public assertion.

Yet, over generations, this choice carried a cost. Without collective rhythm, sacred time gradually slipped from social consciousness. What remained was practice without proclamation, devotion without narrative.

4. When Rivers Fell Out of the Story

As modern infrastructure altered river courses and urban life turned away from natural cycles, rivers themselves fell out of public imagination. When the river is no longer central, river-based sacred time loses its stage. *Bharathapuzha* still flowed, but fewer listened. Maha Magha still arrived, but fewer recognized its footfall.

5. Silence as Dormancy, Not Death

The silence of Maha Magha is not extinction—it is dormancy. Like seeds beneath the soil, sacred time waits for conditions to return. What fell silent did so not from exhaustion, but from dislocation.

This chapter does not mourn loss alone. It recognizes that what withdraws in one age may re-emerge in another, transformed but intact. Maha Magha's silence is therefore not an ending but a pause in expression—awaiting remembrance rather than reconstruction. To listen carefully is to realize: the river still knows the time.

PART V

THE GREAT RETURN (2026)
From Sankalpa to Confluence

CHAPTER 11: THE CALL THAT BECAME A CONFLUENCE

When Intention Found Its Form

The Great Return (2026)—From Saṅkalpa to Confluence

The year 2026 marks more than a calendrical convergence; it signals a civilizational remembering. What once receded into silence now stirs again—not as repetition, but as return with awareness. The Great Return is not driven by spectacle or nostalgia, but by *saṅkalpa*—a conscious resolve to realign time, land, and inner life. As rivers await recognition and memory seeks form, intention moves toward confluence. This section traces how dormant sacred time prepares to flow again—quietly, deliberately, and with purpose—into collective consciousness.

1. Saints, Scholars, Visionaries, Organizers: Many Voices, One Summons

Every civilizational renewal begins not with an institution, but with a call—subtle at first, almost inaudible, arising simultaneously in many hearts. In the years leading to this return, that call stirred saints rooted in silence, scholars immersed in text and tradition, visionaries attuned to the pulse of time, and organizers capable of translating insight into action.

Saints felt it as an inner urgency—a sense that sacred time, long neglected, was seeking recognition. Scholars recognized patterns aligning across calendars, scriptures, and lived traditions. Visionaries perceived a widening gap between ritual memory and modern life and sensed that a bridge was required. Organizers, often unseen yet indispensable, began quietly preparing pathways—logistical, social, and symbolic—for convergence.

None acted alone. None claimed ownership. What united them was a shared intuition: this was not invention, but remembrance. The call was not to create something new, but to allow what had waited patiently to gather again.

2. Swami Anandavanam Bharathi and the Akhāḍā Spirit

Discipline as the Spine of Renewal

At the still centre of this unfolding stood Swami Anandavanam Bharathi, not as a figure of proclamation, but as a presence of steadiness. He embodied the ancient *Akhāḍā* spirit in its truest sense—not as militancy, contest, or display, but as single-pointed resolve aligned with dharma. In its original conception, an *Akhāḍā* is not merely a monastic order; it is a field of consecrated intention, where discipline is sustained collectively and commitment is lived, not announced.

For Swami Anandavanam Bharathi, renunciation was never withdrawal from responsibility. It was its refinement. His *tapas* did not isolate him from the world; it clarified his engagement with it. Carrying the weight of lineage with humility, he represented a continuity that neither fossilized tradition nor diluted it for convenience. The past, in his keeping, remained alive and responsive, not ornamental.

1. Ascetic Resolve with an Open Horizon:

What distinguished Swami Anandavanam Bharathi was the balance he held effortlessly—the firmness of ascetic resolve alongside an expansive, inclusive vision. Deeply grounded in spiritual discipline, mantra, and inherited practice, he nonetheless recognized the realities of the present age. He understood that revival could not be achieved through repetition alone; it required translation without compromise.

Thus, he articulated the return of *Maha Magha* not as a festival to be staged, but as a sacred alignment to be protected. Time, river, people, and intention had to meet in integrity. His guidance gently but firmly redirected energies away from spectacle and toward inner preparedness. Participation was not measured by numbers but by quality of presence.

2. A Trust, Not an Event:

In Swami Anandavanam Bharathi's presence, it became clear that this movement was not an "event" to be organized, advertised, or consumed. It was a trust handed down by time itself. Such a trust demands restraint, vigilance, and accountability—not excitement alone.

This perspective reshaped the entire effort. Decisions were made slowly, with consultation and contemplation. Ritual accuracy mattered. Language was chosen carefully. Silence was honoured as much as speech. Through this, the revival retained its ritual dignity, resisting the modern impulse to convert sacred convergence into performance.

3. Authority Rooted in Authenticity:

Under the *Akhāḍā* spirit he embodied, hierarchy naturally softened. Authority did not assert itself; it was recognized.

Leadership emerged from lived discipline rather than designation. Those who gathered around him felt guided, not commanded.

This atmosphere cultivated mutual respect among saints, scholars, organizers, and householders alike. Each role found its place without rivalry. The *Akhāḍā* ethos acted as a moral compass, ensuring that ego, urgency, or ideological assertion did not fracture the collective intent.

4. Guarding the Revival from Dilution:

Most crucially, this spirit guarded the revival from two great dangers: dilution into sentiment and inflation into spectacle. Discipline prevented excess. Humility prevented appropriation. Dharmic restraint ensured that sacred time was invited, not exploited.

In this way, Swami Anandavanam Bharathi did not "lead" the revival in a conventional sense. He held the centre—allowing others to act while ensuring that the alignment remained true. Through him, the *Akhāḍā* spirit revealed its timeless relevance: that when discipline anchors intention, revival becomes remembrance—not reinvention.

3. Revival as Collective Saṅkalpa: When Will Becomes Sacred

What transformed a call into a confluence was collective *saṅkalpa*. *Saṅkalpa* here was not a slogan or declaration, but a shared interior resolve—renewed each time a person chose participation over passivity, memory over amnesia.

This revival did not depend on mandates or mass mobilization. It grew organically as individuals aligned their intentions: a scholar offering clarity, a priest restoring forgotten rites, a volunteer preparing riverbanks, and a householder adjusting daily life to sacred time. Each act, however small, became a thread in a larger weaving. *Saṅkalpa* turned remembrance into responsibility. It ensured that the return of Maha Magha would not be an imitation of past forms but a living convergence of consciousness, geography, and time.

4. From Call to Confluence

Thus, the call matured into a confluence—not merely of people, but of streams of intent. Saints brought depth, scholars brought coherence, visionaries brought direction, and organizers brought stability. Together, they allowed sacred time to recognize itself once more in human space.

This chapter affirms a timeless truth: when intention is shared and sustained, time responds. Rivers receive. Memory awakens. What had fallen silent does not need to be forced back—it returns when invited with sincerity.

The confluence, therefore, was not manufactured. It was answered.

CHAPTER 12: RESISTANCE, RESOLVE, AND RETURN

History does not always progress through armies or revolutions. At times, it resists through silence, through refusal, through the quiet insistence that something sacred cannot be reduced to a file number. This chapter explores a subtler battlefield—where bureaucracy confronts belief, administration confronts dharma, and spiritual resolve quietly but decisively prevails.

1. Stop Memos and Bureaucratic Resistance

The modern administrative state communicates power not through swords, but through memos, circulars, permissions, and prohibitions. Sacred traditions—especially those rooted in cyclical time, ritual memory, and collective participation—often appear to bureaucracy as inconvenient remnants of the past: unregulated, unpredictable, and resistant to standardization.

"Stop memos" became instruments of interruption. Issued in the language of procedure and public order, they sought to suspend rituals, halt gatherings, and sever continuity under the guise of regulation. What was once a living tradition was reframed as an "event," requiring approval, limitation, or cancellation.

Yet this resistance was not always malicious. It arose from a worldview trained to value control over continuity, efficiency over meaning, and documentation over lived experience. Bureaucracy struggled to comprehend that certain traditions do not begin with permission nor end with prohibition—they exist beyond administrative time.

Ironically, each memo intended to stop a ritual that often reawakened collective memory. What had been taken for granted now had to be defended. What had flowed naturally now demanded conscious protection.

2. Dharma Confronting Administration

The confrontation between dharma and administration is not a clash of violence but of epistemologies—two ways of understanding order.

Administration is linear, rule-bound, and external. Dharma is cyclical, contextual, and internal. Administration asks, "Who *authorized this?"*
Dharma asks, "Who *preserved this across centuries?"*

When dharma confronts administration, it does not shout. It stands firm. Communities invoked precedent older than statutes, legitimacy deeper than paperwork, and authority rooted not in office but in collective conscience.

This was not defiance in the political sense but assertion in the civilizational sense. Elders, scholars, spiritual leaders, and ordinary devotees articulated a powerful truth: that governance exists to serve society, not to erase its soul. Rituals were not disruptions of order—they were the very means through which social harmony had been sustained.

In this moment, dharma revealed its quiet strength. It adapted where necessary, negotiated where possible, but refused to surrender its essence. Administration, accustomed to compliance, encountered something it could neither easily suppress nor fully assimilate—a living tradition anchored in shared faith.

3. The Triumph of Spiritual Resolve

True triumph does not always announce itself dramatically. Often, it unfolds gradually, almost imperceptibly, until one day it becomes undeniable.

Spiritual resolve triumphed not because files were defeated, but because faith outlasted fatigue. Those who stood their ground did so without hatred, without aggression, and without abandoning restraint. Their strength lay in patience, continuity, and moral clarity.

Over time, resistance softened. Memos were revised, permissions granted, and practices resumed—sometimes altered in form, but intact in spirit. More importantly, a deeper recognition emerged: that traditions rooted in dharma cannot be permanently halted by administrative decree.

The return was not merely of a ritual but of confidence—confidence that sacred inheritance, when protected with dignity and resolve, survives even modern disruptions. The episode reaffirmed an enduring civilizational lesson: institutions may govern the present, but dharma governs time itself.

Thus, this chapter stands as a testament—not to conflict, but to convergence—where administration eventually learns to accommodate what it cannot erase, and where spiritual resolve quietly reclaims its rightful place in the flow of history.

CHAPTER 13: THE FIRST FLAME AND THE RISING FLAG

Civilizations do not announce their return solely through proclamations or decrees. They announce themselves through symbols—through fire rekindled, through flags raised, through a collective silence broken by remembrance. Words may declare intent, but symbols awaken memory.

This chapter records such a moment: when time, ritual, and resolve converged, and a tradition long thought dormant re-entered history with quiet, unquestionable authority. What unfolds here is a watershed in spiritual history—the resurgence of an ancient heartbeat that had fallen silent for nearly three centuries. The return of *Maha Magha,* historically remembered in Kerala as *Mamankam,* is not merely the restoration of a festival. It is the realignment of sacred time, the reassertion of *Dharma*, and the invocation of *Agni* as the elemental witness. It marks the point at which remembrance transforms into responsibility, and history yields to continuity. This chapter does not describe an end. It marks a threshold.

1. Nilavilakku as Agni-sākṣi: *The Fire as the Eternal Witness:*

In the Kerala tradition, the *Nilavilakku* is never merely a source of illumination. It is a living presence—a deity in itself. Its lighting is never purely functional; it is a sacramental act that anchors the divine in the material world.

The lamp itself embodies a profound metaphysics, standing as a microcosm of the human experience. Its *brass body*, drawn from the earth, represents the *sthūla śarīra*—the physical vessel. The *oil*, extracted from living seeds, signifies the *manas* and *bhakti*—the mind softened and liquefied by devotion. The *wick* represents *buddhi*, the discriminative intellect, sharp and upright. When the *flame* is finally lit, it signifies the burning away of the ego to reveal the *Ātman* (Soul). What burns is not oil alone, but limitation.

At that instant, the lamp stood at the intersection of the five elements: *Earth* in its form, *Water* in the oil, *Fire* in the flame, *Air* sustaining its rise, and *Space* receiving its light. This is why the first act of the return was not speech, not declaration, and not celebration—but silence before fire.

In Bharatiya consciousness, fire is not a metaphor; it is a witness. *Agni* does not merely illuminate; it testifies. In the Vedic understanding, *Agni* is the messenger between realms, carrying intention upward and memory backward. By invoking *Agni-sākṣi*, the revival of *Maha Magha* was conducted not in secrecy, nor merely in legality, but in the presence of the Elemental God who witnesses vows across lifetimes.

When the *wick* touched the *oil* and the *flame* steadied itself, the moment passed beyond human design and entered cosmic acknowledgement. This specific flame bridged the chasm of centuries. It connected the ancestors (*Pitru*)—who last witnessed the Maha Magha in the eighteenth century—with the generation standing in 2026.

This was the "First Flame" after 270 years of darkness. It was not the darkness of ignorance but the darkness of interruption. Rituals had paused, but the memory had endured in the ether. The flame affirmed continuity beyond rupture. It declared, without a single spoken word: *We have not forgotten. We have returned.*

Just as the sun witnesses the world by day, the *Nilavilakku* witnesses the soul by night. This flame anchored the spiritual energy of all that was to follow. Before the flags rose and the declarations were spoken, the fire had already testified to the truth.

2. Dharma Dhvaja-rohaṇa (January 19, 2026)

1. Ascension of the Flag of Righteousness:

If fire is the soul's witness, the flag is its intention made visible. The date, January 19, 2026, is now etched in the timeline of the spirit as the day of the *Dhvaja-rohaṇa* (Flag Hoisting). In the sacred architecture of the temple and the cosmos, the flagpost (*Dhwajasthambam*) is never merely a structural support; it represents the *Meru Danda*—the spinal column of the cosmic body, the axis around which the universe revolves.

On this day, the *Dharma Dhvaja* was raised—not as a political emblem, nor as a banner of territorial conquest, but as a sublime declaration of alignment. In the *Sanātana* tradition, a *dhvaja* announces a divine presence: it proclaims, "*Dharma* is awake here." It signals to the visible and invisible worlds that a space has been reconsecrated, that a lineage has reclaimed its voice, and that the silence is over.

As the flag ascended, it cut through more than just the air; it pierced layers of historical amnesia. For nearly three centuries, the pole had stood absent, the sky above the Nila River unmarked by this specific assertion of duty. Now, as cloth met wind and colour met light, the horizon itself seemed to acknowledge the return.

There was no roar of aggression, no triumphal excess. The

power of the moment lay in its restraint. Elders watched in deep reverence, while younger generations watched in astonishment, sensing that they were witnessing not an event, but a restoration. The *Dharma Dhvaja-rohaṇa* re-established the sacred geography, reminding all present that *Dharma* does not vanish—it waits for the righteous to hoist it once more.

2. The Rising Kundalini: A Signal to the Universe:

The hoisting of the flag is a mirror of the internal spiritual process. Just as the *Kundalini Shakti* rises from the base of the spine to the crown, the flag ascends the *Dhwajasthambam*.

1. *The External Yajna:* As the flag reached its zenith, it acted as a signal to the universe. It confirmed that the *Yajna* (the great offering) had begun. The fluttering of the flag represents the *Spanda* (divine vibration)—the heartbeat of a culture coming back to life.

2. *The Collective Consciousness:* This was not the act of a single individual, but the rising of the collective consciousness of a society. The flag represents the shared aspiration of the people to rise above the mundane and touch the divine.

3. From Yuddha to Dharma: The Great Transmutation:

To understand the magnitude of this flag hoisting, one must understand the shadow of the past.

1. *Healing History:* Historically, the *Mamankam* was synonymous with martial prowess, the clashing of steel, and the deadly resolve of the *Chaver Pada* (suicide squads) challenging the Zamorin. It was a festival of power and blood.

2. *The Shift:* The 2026 revival signifies a profound transmutation. The raising of the *Dharma Dhvaja* shifts the focus from *Yuddha* (War) to *Dharma* (Cosmic Order). It

declares that the new era is not about conquering land, but about conquering the self. The flag does not claim territory; it claims a return to spiritual roots. It is a peace offering to history, transforming the trauma of the past into the sanctity of the present.

4. The Auspicious Alignment: Uttarayana:

The timing of this act was divinely ordained.

1. *The Path of Light:* January corresponds to *Uttarayana*—the northward movement of the sun. In Vedic science, this is the "Day of the Gods," a time when the solar energy is ascending and conducive to spiritual growth.

2. *The Vertical Axis:* January 19th marked a specific celestial alignment where the energies were ripe for inception. By hoisting the flag during this window, a vertical axis was created, connecting *Bhu* (Earth) to *Svarga* (Heaven). This axis acts as a lightning rod for divine grace, creating a protected, consecrated field for the rituals of the *Maha Magha* to unfold.

3. The Declaration of Maha Magha's Return After 270 Years

This moment serves as the chapter's crescendo—a peak where history and destiny collide. To fully grasp the magnitude of this return, we must look beyond the festivities and understand the 270-year "silence" that enveloped the banks of the *Nila*.

1. The Philosophy of "Return" vs. Revival":

The most critical distinction in this declaration is linguistic and metaphysical: the event is a return, not a revival.

1. *Revival (Resurrection):* This implies that something had died, decayed, and ceased to exist, requiring an external force to bring it back to life. It suggests a break in the lineage.

2. *Return (Continuity):* This implies that the essence never left; it merely went underground. Like a river that flows beneath the surface during a drought only to spring forth when the rains return, *Maha Magha* remained latent.

The Latency of Tradition: The festival was preserved in the collective memory of the region, in the oral traditions of the elders, and in the "longing" of the land itself. The formal announcement was simply the physical manifestation of a spiritual flame that had been kept burning in secret.

2. The Historical Context: The 270-Year Silence

To understand the relief of the return, one must understand the pain of the cessation. The text refers to a "rupture caused by history."

1. *The Cessation (c. 1755–1766):* The ancient *Mamankam* was a grand assembly held every 12 years on the banks of the *Bharathapuzha* (River Nila) in *Tirunavaya*. It halted due to severe geopolitical upheaval in the Malabar region—specifically the Mysore invasions (Hyder Ali and Tipu Sultan), followed by the consolidation of British power.

2. *The Loss of Patronage:* The festival was historically anchored by the Zamorin (*Samoothiri*) of Calicut. When the political structures crumbled, the logistical ability to host such a massive event vanished.

3. *The Great Dormancy:* For nearly three centuries, the "Great Year" cycle was broken physically. However, the declaration argues that Sacred Time (*Kala*) operates independently of Political Time. Governments fell, borders shifted, and wars were fought, but the 12-year cosmic rhythm continued to tick silently, waiting for society to realign with it.

3. The Transformation: From Feud to Healing:

The return is not a blind repetition of the past; it is an evolution.

3.1. The Healing of Karma (Dosha):

The ancient *Mamankams* were legendary for their grandeur, but they were also marred by blood. They were the stage for the *Chaver Pada* (suicide squads) of the *Valluvanad* Raja, who sought to avenge the honour of their lineage against the Zamorin.

1. *Then*: The river witnessed vendettas, martial dominance, and death.

2. *Now* (2026): The return transforms the *Dosha* (blemish) of that violence. The 2026 return is a *Sankalpa* (solemn resolve) to convert a site of conflict into a site of confluence. It replaces the sword with the prayer lamp.

3.2 Re-opening the Civilizational Rhythm:

The text beautifully notes that this is the "reopening of a civilizational rhythm." In Hindu cosmology, rituals act as the heartbeat of a civilization. When the heartbeat stops, the civilization drifts.

The Responsibility: The declaration shifts the narrative from "inheriting a festival" to "accepting a responsibility." It affirms that the current generation is now the custodian of a legacy that survived 270 years of darkness to reach them.

4. Summary of the Cycle Closing:

The long era between 1755 and 2025 may be understood as a period of sacred silence. During these centuries, the tradition did not disappear; it remained latent—carefully preserved in memory, scripture, and collective longing. What existed was not living practice but remembrance: a sense of what once had been. The absence of ritual created a void in time, where tradition survived inwardly rather than being expressed outwardly. Emotionally, this period was marked by nostalgia and quiet yearning, as generations carried forward the memory without the means to fully enact it.

From 2026 onward, a decisive transition occurs—from latency to manifestation. The tradition re-enters life as a living reality, consciously reclaimed through ritual, action, and collective resolve. What was once only remembered is now enacted. The dominant emotional tone shifts from longing to humility and responsibility, accompanied by a firm resolve to sustain what has been restored. The river, which had silently witnessed neglect and displacement, now becomes an active participant in purification and unity, transforming from a passive observer into a sacred collaborator.

Spiritually, the goal also undergoes a profound elevation. During the era of silence, the foremost aim was survival—the safeguarding of memory against erasure. In the era of return, the aspiration expands beyond preservation toward fulfillment: *moksha* and collective unity. The tradition no longer seeks merely to endure time but to transcend it, guiding the community from remembrance to liberation and from historical survival to spiritual wholeness.

Conclusion: The Conscious Re-entry

The declaration of *Maha Magha's* return is the closing of a massive karmic loop. It proves the resilience of spiritual geography—that land (the Nila) and water retain memory longer than human records do. By framing this as a return with awareness, the declaration invites the participants not to merely act out old scripts but to enter the river with the humility of those who know how easily tradition can be lost and the resolve of those determined to never let the flame go out again.

PART VI

RITUALS OF THE SOUL The Inner Experience of Maha Magha

CHAPTER 14: MAGHA SNĀNA—THE SOUTHERN HOLY DIP

The Inner Experience of Maha Magha

While *Maha Magha* is often perceived through the spectacle of its external forms—the lit lamps, raised flags, and gathering crowds—its true essence lies in a subtler pilgrimage that unfolds within the human heart. This section shifts the narrative gaze inward, framing the festival not merely as a public observance but as an intimate spiritual alignment where ritual serves as a language for the self to converse with the eternal. In the *Sanātana* vision, every vow taken and step toward the river mirrors an internal movement from fragmentation to coherence, transforming collective commemoration into personal awakening. Serving as the spiritual anchor of the text, this chapter moves from the weight of history to the immediacy of individual experience, focusing on the *Snāna* (Holy Dip) not as a physical cleansing, but as a profound metaphysical event where memory becomes meaning and time dissolves into presence.

1. The Context: The Sanctity of the South (*Dakshina Ganga*)

To understand the *Magha Snāna* in this narrative, one must first reorient one's spiritual geography. While the collective consciousness of India often turns toward the Triveni Sangam in Prayagraj (Northern India) for the holy dip, this chapter asserts a powerful reclamation of the South. It posits that the *Bharathapuzha (Nila)* is not merely a regional waterway but the *Dakshina Ganga*—the Ganges of the South.

Why the "Southern" Dip?

While *Magha Snāna* is famously associated with the Triveni Sangam in Prayagraj (Northern India), this chapter reclaims the sanctity of the South. It establishes the *Bharathapuzha (Nila)* as the *Dakshina Ganga* (Southern Ganges). This section establishes three pillars of validity for the Southern Dip:

A. The Geospiritual Reclaiming:

The text challenges the notion that sanctity is confined to the Himalayas or the Gangetic plains. It establishes the Nila River as a spiritual mirror to the Ganges. Just as the Ganges nurtures the civilization of the North, the Nila has been the silent matriarch of the Kerala civilization, absorbing the prayers, ashes, and history of the region for millennia. By invoking the title *Dakshina Ganga*, the narrative reminds the devotee that the divine current flows with equal potency in the South.

B. The Celestial Alignment (*Kala*):

The sanctity of the dip is not arbitrary; it is governed by cosmic geometry.

1. The Month of Magha: The ritual occurs during the auspicious lunar month of *Magha* (typically spanning January–February).

2. The Solar Transit: This period coincides with the Sun's entry into Capricorn (*Makara Rashi*). In Vedic astronomy, this transition marks the dawn of the "day of the gods" (*Uttarayana*).

3. The Confluence: The text explains that during this specific astronomical window, the water in the Nila is believed to be charged with heightened cosmic energy, transforming it from H_2O into *Amrita* (nectar).

C. The Law of Equivalence:

Perhaps the most profound assertion is the metaphysical equivalence of the waters.

1. Water as a Single Entity: The text argues that in the spiritual vision, all sacred waters are one. The vibrational capacity of the water to heal the spirit is absolute, regardless of latitude.

2. The Resolution: Whether one dips in the freezing waters of Prayagraj or the flowing currents of the Nila, the spiritual result—*Papa Pariharam* (remission of sins) and *Chitta Shuddhi* (purification of the mind)—is identical. The geography changes, but the grace remains constant.

2. Emotional Dimensions: The Dissolution of Ego

To step into the river during the month of Magha is to step into the currents of one's own unfinished history. Water is the great equalizer; it carries no judgment, asks for no credentials, and demands no explanations. Yet, as it touches the skin, it evokes everything that lies beneath the surface of the persona—grief long suppressed, vows half-remembered, and the silent burdens carried across lifetimes.

The *Magha Snāna* is not merely a ritual obligation; it is a profound act of emotional surrender. It is the dismantling of the "I."

A. The Cold Awakening: The Shock of the Now:

The experience begins with the visceral reality of the element. The waters of the Nila in the month of Magha are piercingly cold.

This thermal shock serves a spiritual function: it instantly snaps the devotee out of the hypnosis of mental chatter (*chitta vritti*). The shock bypasses the intellect and forces the consciousness into a state of acute, vibrating presence.

The Shift: In that shivering moment, the anxieties of the future and the regrets of the past evaporate. There is no timeline—there is only the water, the breath, and the Now.

B. The Great Equalizer: Vulnerability and the Naked Self:

To enter the river, one must strip away the costumes of the world. Standing waist-deep in the current, the distinctions of hierarchy vanish. King and pauper, priest and rebel, elder and child—all stand shivering and equal before the majesty of nature.

The Unmasking: The water strips away social masks and accumulated titles, leaving only the raw, vulnerable human spirit. This vulnerability is the gateway to grace. Many enter the water with folded hands and lowered eyes, not in a posture of defeat, but in the strength of surrender.

C. The Fluidity of Karma: Reorienting the Soul:

In the *Sanātana* vision, karma is not a system of punishment but of momentum—the kinetic energy of past actions seeking resolution. *Magha Snāna* offers a sacred pause in this momentum. It does not magically erase the past, but it reorients the future.

The Release: Repentance here is not confessional; it is contemplative. The devotee does not narrate sins to a judge; they release attachments to the mother. The water becomes a medium through which unresolved impressions (*saṃskāras*) are acknowledged and gently loosened. Tears and river water become indistinguishable, flowing together to carry away not guilt, but weight. Just as the river bends around obstacles without breaking, the soul, touched by this awareness, learns to shift its course toward the ocean of Truth.

D. The Maternal Embrace: Returning to the Source:

Above all, Nila is addressed as *Amma* (Mother). The dip is an emotional return to the cosmic womb. In the suspension of the water, the devotee feels held, rocked, and embraced by a force larger than themselves.

The Healing: This tactile embrace triggers a release of deep-seated grief and offers a sense of profound safety. It is a moment of filial gratitude that bridges the individual life with the ancestral line. The remembered and the forgotten, the fulfilled and the restless—all are symbolically invited into the current, healing the lineage through the piety of the living.

3. Karmic Dimensions: The Washing of the Subtle Body

In the profound vision of Hindu philosophy, the physical body is merely a vessel. Housed within it is the *Sukshma Sharira* (the subtle body), which carries the imprint of every thought, action, and unfulfilled desire across lifetimes. This accumulated weight is known as Karma—often visualized as spiritual dust that dims the natural brilliance of the Soul (*Atman*). The *Magha Snāna* is the celestial mechanism for removing this dust. It is an act of spiritual alchemy where the heavy is exchanged for the light.

A. The Transfer of Burden:

The River Nila is revered because she possesses the infinite capacity to absorb *Papa* (transgressions) without ever becoming impure herself. When the devotee dips beneath the surface, a profound visualization takes place: they imagine their negative karma—their guilt, anger, and accumulated errors—flowing out of their pores and into the current. The water accepts this burden willingly, carrying it away to the ocean, leaving the devotee cleansed not just in body but in spirit.

B. The Bridge to Ancestors* (Rina)*:

We do not walk this earth alone; we carry the biology and the karma of those who came before us. The holy dip is inextricably linked to *Pitru Tarpanam* (oblations to ancestors). The river acts as a mystic conduit between the living and the departed. By bathing in these waters, the devotee performs an act of filial gratitude, soothing the restless spirits of their lineage and paying off the *Rina* (karmic debt). It is a healing of the family tree, ensuring that the blessings of the ancestors flow forward rather than their burdens.

C. The Spiritual Reset:

The moment of emerging from the water is nothing short of a rebirth. As the devotee breaks the surface and gasps for air, it symbolizes a clean break from the past. The "Old Self," with its heavy entanglements, has been washed downstream. The "New Self" steps onto the riverbank purified, lighter, and ready to begin the cycle of life again—not with the weight of history, but with the clarity of the present.

4. The Triad of Water: Purifier, Witness, Liberator

In the sacred geography of *Sanātana Dharma*, water (*Jala*) is never merely a physical element; it is a sentient force. It is *Āpaḥ*—the primordial waters, the first medicine, the fluid that precedes form and sustains life.

During the holy month of Magha, the river is not observed as a passive resource but revered as a conscious presence. It interacts with the devotee through three distinct, metaphysical roles.

A. Water as Purifier (Shuddhi):

The first role of the river is purification, but this transcends the simple hygiene of the body.

1. *The Inner Cleansing:* While the water washes away physical grime, its true target is the *Antahkarana* (the inner conscience). The immersion represents the washing away of *mala*—spiritual obscuration. Just as dust settles invisibly on a mirror over time, emotional residues and cynicisms settle over the mind. *Magha Snāna* is the ritual moment when these accumulations are acknowledged and released.

2. *The Vibrational Charge:* The water of the Nila is believed to be more than H_2O; it is a storage medium for memory. It carries the magnetic charge of thousands of years of sages' prayers (*tapasya*) performed on its banks. To dip into the river is to realign one's own chaotic bio-magnetic field with this ancient, stabilized frequency.

B. Water as Witness (Sakshi):

In Vedic rituals, fire (*Agni*) is usually the witness to our vows, but water is the witness to our surrender.

1. *The Silent Historian:* The River Nile is the oldest historian of the land. It has watched the grand Mamankams of the 12th century; it witnessed the bloodshed of the invasions; it flowed through the 270-year silence; and now, it watches the Return. When one enters the river, one enters this long memory.

2. *The Ultimate Mirror:* You cannot hide from the water. It touches every inch of the skin and envelops the body entirely. It knows the difference between a dip performed out of hollow routine and one performed with a trembling heart. It serves as the ultimate, unbiased witness to the devotee's true intent (*Sankalpa*).

*C. Water as Liberator (***Moksha Dayini***):*

Finally, the river performs its subtlest function: it teaches the soul how to be free.

1. *The Model of the Soul:* The river's physical journey models the soul's spiritual trajectory. Just as the Nila relentlessly flows toward the ocean, seeking to lose its name and form in the vastness of the sea, the individual soul seeks to lose its ego and merge with the Divine (*Brahman*).

2. *The Rehearsal:* The dip is a gentle rehearsal for the ultimate dissolution. To immerse fully—to hold one's breath and go under—is to practice the art of letting go. In that moment of suspension, the body yields, and the fear of separation loosens. The water teaches that liberation is not an escape from the world but a reconciliation with it—flowing, trusting, and merging.

5. The Southern Sacred Current: A Sanctuary of Intimacy

To understand the unique spiritual vibration of the Southern *Magha Snāna*, one must appreciate the distinction between **power** and **presence.**

While the great gatherings of the North—at Prayagraj or Haridwar—are defined by their sheer magnitude, the roar of millions, and the overwhelming sensory overload of divinity, the experience on the banks of the Nila is defined by its intimacy. It is less proclaimed, yet no less profound.

A. The Geography of Quietude:

Here, the sacred does not shout; it whispers. The festival does not seek to overwhelm the senses with spectacle but to envelop the soul in silence. The crowds are not a sea of strangers but a gathering of kin. In this southern sanctuary, the distance between the devotee and the Divine is collapsed not by the grandeur of the ritual, but by the quietude of the environment. The river is not a stage for performance; it is a secluded room for prayer.

B. Mother, Not Monument:

The text draws a vital distinction: in the South, the river is experienced as Mother, not Monument.

1. *The Monument:* A monument is static, distant, and demands awe. It is something to be looked at.

2. *The Mother:* A mother is dynamic, accessible, and offers comfort. She is someone to be held by.

The Nila is not approached as a deity to be appeased from afar but as a companion who walks alongside the history of the land. She is the keeper of secrets and the washer of sorrows. The relationship is not transactional ("I give this, you give that"); it is relational ("I am here, and you are holding me").

C. The Theology of Consent:

Perhaps the most profound shift in this chapter is the redefinition of the dip itself.

1. *Conquest vs. Consent:* In many spiritual pursuits, there is a language of "conquest"—conquering the mind, conquering the senses. But here, the pilgrim does not conquer the river. The pilgrim consents to be held by it.

2. *The Buoyancy of Faith:* This physical act mirrors a spiritual truth: just as one cannot float in water if they are thrashing and fighting, one cannot find peace in God through rigid effort alone. One must relax. One must trust the water to bear the weight.

This consent marks the pivotal turning point of the inner journey—the shift from *Sadhana* (spiritual effort) to *Sharanagati* (absolute surrender).

D. From Remembering to Releasing

The immersion completes the cycle.

1. The Entry: We enter the water remembering our ancestors, our mistakes, and our desires.

2. The Exit: We emerge, releasing. The current takes what we no longer need to carry.

The journey moves from the tension of "doing" to the grace of "being." In the gentle, flowing arms of the Nila, the devotee realizes that they do not need to fight the current of time; they only need to learn how to swim within it.

CHAPTER 15: NILA ĀRATI—WHEN FIRE MET WATER

The twilight descends upon the banks of the *Nila* not as darkness, but as a violet hush. The air is thick, saturated with the earthy petrichor of river mud mixed with the sharp, cleansing fragrance of burning camphor and sandalwood oil. Here, beside the *Bharatapuzha* (the River Nila)—the lifeline that flows through the heart of Kerala's culture—a ritual takes place that is less of a performance and more of a cosmic alignment.

The Nila is often described as calm yet strong, silently watching traditions fade and sands dry. But in this moment, she stands majestic. This ceremony brings together sky and earth, gently linking the divine above with the world below through a glow of sacred light.

1. When Fire Met Water: The Primordial Union

"In the syntax of the universe, fire is the rising prayer, and water is the descending grace."

This section explores the alchemical reaction between two opposing elements. In the physical world, water extinguishes fire. In the spiritual world, they consummate a sacred union.

1. The Descent of Light (The Active Principle):

As the priest raises the heavy brass lamp, the flame becomes a living entity.

The Mirror of the Soul: The flame is held over the dark, flowing water. It does not just illuminate the surface; it penetrates the depths. This act symbolizes the *Jivatma* (the individual soul) —fiery, restless, constantly consuming, and striving upward— offering itself to the *Paramatma* (the Supreme Soul), represented by the river.

The Dance: The flame flickers in the river breeze. It is a dance of vulnerability. The fire risks extinction to be close to the water, just as the devotee risks the dissolution of the ego to be close to the Divine.

2. The Hiss of Extinction (The Silent Tension):

There is a profound metaphysical tension here.

Agni (Fire): The Devourer, the sacred force of time and transformation that consumes illusion, decay, and ego—ending what no longer serves dharma so that truth, renewal, and rebirth may arise. Agni transforms everything it touches into ash and smoke (spirit). It is the Unmoving Witness, the intense focus of meditation.

Jala (Water): The Sustainer, the life-giving force that preserves balance, nurtures continuity, and upholds harmony by sustaining all that is righteous, living, and aligned with dharma. Jala flows, changes, and nourishes. It is the ever-changing world (Samsara).

The Meeting Point: When the heat of the camphor hits the cool aura of the river, the boundary dissolves. It signifies that the heat of human suffering is cooled only by the grace of the cosmic flow.

2. Kashi-Inspired, Yet Kerala-Rooted

"The ancient chants of Varanasi find a new dialect in the verdant silence of the South."

This ritual, Nila Arati, is an act of spiritual translation. It takes the "software" of the North Indian Ganga Aarti and runs it on the "hardware" of Kerala's unique culture.

1. The Kashi Spectacle (The Macrocosm):

The inspiration comes from the legendary ghats of Kashi (Varanasi).

Grandeur and Geometry: Like in Kashi, the movements are large and sweeping. The lamps are not just waved; they trace the *Omkara* (the symbol of Om) and the *Chakra* (the wheel of time) in the air.

The River as Goddess: In Kashi, she is Mother Ganga. Here, she is Nila Devi. The ritual acknowledges that the river is a conscious, living entity that demands a royal audience, requiring the priests to wear the silks of purity and hold the posture of warriors guarding a treasure.

2. The Kerala Soul (The Microcosm):

However, the flavour is distinctly Malayali. The aesthetics shift from the gold and glitter of the North to the wood, brass, and fire of the South.

The Aesthetic: Instead of the multi-tiered, ornate *Deepams* of the North, the *Nila Ārati* often utilizes the *Nilavilakku* (the floor lamp) or the *Thookkuvilakku* (hanging lamp). These lamps have a stark, architectural beauty—simple curves of bronze that speak of stability and ancient heritage rather than opulence.

The Atmosphere: Varanasi is a cacophony—a chaotic explosion of bells and shouts. The Nila, conversely, is steeped in a poetic silence. The crowd here does not cheer; they fold their hands. The backdrop is not stone palaces but swaying coconut palms and the wet sands of *Thirunavaya* or Ponnani. It is an intimate whisper to the divine, grounded in humility.

3. Tantric Rhythm, Lamps, and Cosmic Dialogue:

"Sound is the body of the drum; light is the body of the lamp; Silence is the body of God."

The architecture of this worship is built upon *Tantra*—the weaving of energy through instrument, gesture, and focus.

1. The Tantric Rhythm (The Heartbeat):

The soundscape is not mere accompaniment; it is a technology of consciousness.

The Percussion: The rhythm follows the *Tala* of the universe. The *Chenda* (cylindrical drum) cracks through the air like lightning, awakening the senses. The *Mizhavu* (copper pot drum) offers a deep, womb-like resonance.

The Mechanic of Energy: The priest moves his arm in sync with this beat. He becomes a conduit. The rhythmic clanging creates a *Spanda* (primordial vibration) that forces the chatter of the human mind to stop, aligning the devotee's heartbeat with the current of the river.

2. The Lamps as Yantras:

The lamps are treated as *Yantras*—geometric machines of energy.

Cleansing the Ether: As the lamps rotate clockwise, they are believed to act as a centrifuge. They spin out *Tamas* (the energy of lethargy, darkness, and inertia) from the atmosphere and pull in *Sattva* (clarity, light, and purity).

The Circle: The circle has no beginning and no end. By tracing it with fire, the priest mimics the orbit of planets, reminding the viewer that human life is part of a larger, cyclical order.

3. The Cosmic Dialogue (The Crescendo):

This is the final movement, where dualities merge. The chanting stops. The drums fade into a hum.

The Reflection: The river, now dark as ink, reflects two things: the distant stars in the sky and the fire in the priest's hand. For a fleeting second, the stars and the fire look identical.

Tat Tvam Asi: The devotee gazes into the water. They see their own reflection, backlit by the holy fire. The realization strikes: *The light is not just in the lamp. The light is not just in the star. The light is in me.*

The Conclusion: The camphor burns out, leaving a lingering scent. The fire has "died" into the ether, but the water continues to flow. The conversation ends not with an answer, but with a state of being—peace.

CHAPTER 16: PITṚ YAJÑA—REMEMBERING THE UNREMEMBERED

Nila's banks *Pitṛ Yajña* is the sacred discipline of remembrance offered to those who came before us—ancestors, unnamed forebears, and forgotten souls whose silent lives shaped the present. In the Vedic vision, human existence is never isolated or self-generated; it flows within an unbroken continuum of memory, responsibility, and gratitude. This *yajña* restores that continuity, reminding the living that they stand upon invisible foundations laid by countless lives, remembered and unremembered alike.

In the Vedic perspective, existence is not a singular event that commences at birth and concludes at death. It is a single moment within an infinite current of existence. *Pitṛ Yajña*—the Sacrifice to the Ancestors—is one of the *Pancha Maha Yajñas* prescribed for the householder, affirming that the present is built upon the quiet endurance and sacrifice of the past. This chapter is a call to stand at the water's edge—both literal and symbolic—to look backward with reverence so that we may move forward with clarity.

1. The Vedic Context: Ṛṇa—The Sacred Debt

To understand *Pitṛ Yajña*, one must first understand the Vedic concept of *Ṛṇa*—sacred debt. The scriptures teach that every human being is born carrying three inherent obligations:

1. *Deva Ṛṇa:* the debt to the divine forces for the gifts of nature—sun, air, rain, and earth.

2. *Ṛṣi Ṛṇa:* the debt to the sages for knowledge, wisdom, and cultural continuity.

3. *Pitṛ Ṛṇa:* the debt to the ancestors for the physical body, lineage, and social inheritance.

Pitṛ Yajña is the ethical and spiritual means of repaying this third debt. It is not ancestor worship in a narrow sense but an act of cosmic gratitude. In the *Rig Veda*, the *Pitṛs* are not feared spirits but benevolent guardians—*Pathikṛt,* those who have prepared the path to the other world.

Spiritual Insight: We carry our ancestors in our very marrow. We carry their struggles, resilience, and unfulfilled aspirations within us. To ignore them is to deny the roots of one's own existence.

2. Ancestor Rites: Gratitude Beyond Memory

Ancestor rites are performed not only for those whose names we remember but for the entire ancestral stream. Through offerings of water (*tarpana*), food (*piṇḍa dāna*), and sacred mantras, the living acknowledge an unseen but enduring debt. These rituals affirm that ancestry extends beyond bloodlines to include teachers, protectors, caretakers, and all who upheld and transmitted dharma. *Pitṛ Yajña* thus becomes an act of humility—an acknowledgment that sacrifices sustain one's life made long before one's birth.

The Inner Science of Tarpana:

The central ritual of this chapter is *Tarpana,* meaning "to satiate." Visualize the act: standing in a flowing river or holding a copper vessel, one mixes water (*jala*), black sesame seeds (*til*), and sometimes sacred *kuśa* grass. The water is then allowed to flow gently through the fingers as the mind rests on the departed.

1. *Water* represents life, emotion, and continuity, bridging the gross and the subtle worlds.

2. *Sesame* seeds symbolize preservation of energy and the dissolution of impurities.

3. *Direction* matters: *Pitṛ* rites face south, the direction of *Yama,* signalling a conscious engagement with mortality and justice.

When the word *"Svadhā"* is uttered, a subtle message is sent: *May you be at peace. May you be healed. May your journey toward light continue.*

3. Fallen Warriors and Forgotten Souls

Pitṛ Yajña extends beyond family lineage to embrace fallen warriors, displaced communities, and victims of famine, conflict, and injustice—souls erased from written history yet embedded in the land itself. Many died without rites, remembrance, or closure. Ritual remembrance restores dignity to these lives, acknowledging their suffering and courage. In this sense, *Pitṛ Yajña* becomes a civilizational act.

This chapter expands the ritual horizon toward a profound ethical imperative: remembering the unremembered. After massive upheavals—such as the Kurukshetra war of the *Mahābhārata*—countless individuals perish without name, kin, or funeral rites. These are the *Avīra*, those without descendants, and those taken suddenly by violence.

The Spiritual Crisis of Forgetting:

In Vedic thought, souls who die abruptly (*durmaraṇa*) or without remembrance may linger in intermediate realms, bound by unresolved trauma. They are not "hungry" for food, but for acknowledgment.

Ritual as Rescue:

This chapter describes offerings made not only for one's parents but also for:

1. the soldier who died alone on a battlefield,
2. the victim of disease with no one to mourn them,
3. even the fallen "enemy," whose soul too seeks peace.

This is the summit of Vedic ethics—compassion that transcends death, identity, and enmity. By offering water to the unknown soul, the practitioner becomes the family they never had.

4. Healing Historical Memory Through Ritual

Ritual accomplishes what history books often cannot—it heals. *Pitṛ Yajña* allows individuals and societies to confront suppressed grief without blame or bitterness. By choosing remembrance over resentment, ritual transforms pain into reconciliation. Memory becomes wisdom, not a wound.

Why does such an act matter today? History is not static; it is dynamic.

Unresolved pasts leave imprints—what modern psychology calls intergenerational trauma and the Vedas call *saṁskāras*. When loss is buried rather than mourned, it resurfaces as unrest, fear, and repetition of violence.

Pitṛ Yajña functions as collective therapy:

1. *Acknowledgment* – "You were here. You mattered."
2. *Release*—grief is symbolically washed away.
3. *Integration*—lessons are retained without carrying the pain.

Conclusion: Custodians of Memory

Pitṛ Yajña is not a backward-looking ritual but a forward-moving one. By honoring the unremembered, it restores moral balance and strengthens collective identity. It teaches that we are custodians of historical memory. Forgetting the sacrifices of builders, warriors, mothers, farmers, and unnamed lives is akin to disrupting the cosmic chain.

By performing *Pitṛ Yajña*, we do not drag the past into the present; we heal the past so the future may be free. We transform the ghosts of history into guardians of lineage.

पृथिवी नः सौम्या भवतु ।
पितरः नः प्रसन्नाः सन्तु ।
मा नः जीवनसूत्रात् विच्छेदः भूयात् ॥

Pṛthivī naḥ saumya bhavatu |

Pitaraḥ naḥ prasannāḥ santu |

Mā naḥ jīvana-sūtrāt vicchedaḥ bhūyāt ||

"May the earth be gentle to us, may the ancestors be gracious to us.

May we never be severed from the thread of life."
— ***Rig Veda***

Solemn Ritual Closing Mantra for Pitṛ Yajña:

स्वधा स्वधा पितृभ्यो नमः ।
तृप्ताः सन्तु पितरः सर्वे दृश्याऽदृश्याश्च ये ।
अस्माकं कुले धर्मो वर्धतां शान्तिरेव च ।

कृतं पितृयज्ञकर्मेदं पूर्णं भवतु शाश्वतम् ॥

Svadhā Svadhā Pitṛbhyo Namaḥ

Tṛptāḥ Santu Pitaraḥ Sarve Dṛśyā'dṛśyāśca Ye

Asmākaṁ Kule Dharmo Vardhatāṁ Śāntir Eva Ca

Kṛtaṁ Pitṛ-Yajña-Karmedaṁ Pūrṇaṁ Bhavatu Śāśvatam

Svadhā, svadhā—salutations to the ancestors.

May all ancestors, known and unknown, be satisfied.

May dharma and peace flourish in our lineage.

May this Pitṛ Yajña be complete and eternally fulfilled.

PART VII

LIVING MYTHOLOGY When the Sacred Walked Again

CHAPTER 17: WHEN MYTH WALKED AMONG PEOPLE

After centuries of silence, *Maha Magha* returned not as a distant memory or preserved legend, but as a living presence, reviving an ancient rhythm in which time, river, and ritual once again flowed as one. This return marked a rare historical moment when mythology stepped out of scripture and into lived experience, reminding the South that the sacred never vanishes —it waits, and when time ripens, it walks among people. At such moments, myth ceases to be symbolic or remote and becomes visible, audible, and participatory; the boundary between the remembered past and the living present dissolves, and stories of "long ago" begin to breathe through human lives. In the Vedic and Indic vision, myth (*Purāṇa*) is not falsehood but truth expressed in a form vast enough to be lived and remembered history seen through the lens of consciousness rather than chronology. This chapter traces those luminous epochs when the divine was no longer distant or abstract but walked barefoot upon the earth, collapsing the gap between human and sacred and transforming belief into direct encounter, where myth moved among people as lived reality.

1. Saints, Seekers, Stories: The Living Scriptures

At the heart of every living myth stand saints and seekers—

those who embody truth rather than merely speak about it. They do not arrive proclaiming themselves as legends; they appear as wanderers, renunciants, householders, or pilgrims, moving quietly through the world. Yet their presence alters the atmosphere around them. Ordinary spaces—riverbanks, huts, streets, and marketplaces—are transformed into sacred geography simply by the depth of awareness they carry. In their lives, memory awakens, and the past breathes again.

Reactivating Myth Through Life:

Such saints do not invent myths; they reactivate them. Through silence, compassion, discipline, and conduct, ancient narratives find renewed expression. When a saint walks along a river, it recalls the footsteps of sages of earlier ages. When a seeker listens with humility and surrender, the timeless dialogue between guru and disciple resumes. Myth does not return through spectacle or proclamation, but through authenticity. It lives again when truth is lived, not performed.

1. The Saint as Living Scripture:

We often imagine scriptures as texts—ink fixed on fragile pages. The Vedic tradition, however, affirms that the highest scripture is the realized being (*Jīvanmukta*). Figures such as Ramakrishna Paramahamsa, Ramana Maharshi, or Mirabai did not merely teach philosophy; they demonstrated it through their lives. They became "walking myths," reenacting eternal cosmic truths in human form. When Hanuman serves Rama, it remains a story, but when a devotee serves the poor with the same selfless intensity, the archetype of Hanuman descends into flesh and blood. The myth becomes embodied.

2. The Seeker as Participant:

In this living tradition, the seeker is never a passive observer. Each listener, pilgrim, or disciple becomes an active participant in the divine play (*Līlā*). The lives and stories of saints do not place divinity on a distant pedestal; they reveal it as a latent possibility within the human heart. Saints serve as mirrors, reflecting not what they alone are, but what humanity itself can become. Through them, mythology ceases to belong to the past and enters the present as a lived, unfolding reality.

2. Oral Traditions Reborn: The Breath of Truth

Long before scripture was fixed in writing, truth travelled through voice, gesture, and living memory. Oral traditions were the primary vessels through which mythology remained alive —fluid rather than rigid, responsive rather than static, and deeply rooted in lived experience. This section traces how such traditions naturally re-emerge when the time is ripe, reminding us that the sacred does not depend solely on text but on transmission.

Around sacred gatherings, riverbanks, and pilgrim paths, stories arise almost effortlessly—sung, narrated, or softly shared. Elders recall fragments once received from their elders; wandering ascetics and minstrels revive verses long thought forgotten. These narratives are never repeated word for word. They breathe, shift, and respond to the needs of the moment. In retelling, mythology sheds formality and regains intimacy, becoming once again something felt rather than merely known.

Through oral transmission, the sacred is not learned as information—it is remembered as inheritance. Myth becomes collective memory, not distant authority. In the Vedic tradition, wisdom was preserved as *Śruti*—that which is heard. This was not a technological limitation but a conscious choice, affirming that certain truths must pass through living breath to remain alive.

1. Śabda: The Power of Sound:

In Vedic understanding, sound (*śabda*) carries *prāṇa*, the life force of the speaker. Knowledge spoken by a realized being carries the vibration of lived truth. When a story is told orally, it enters not only through the ears but also through the heart, shaping consciousness rather than merely informing the mind.

2. Tradition as Renewal, Not Repetition:

Oral traditions—folk tales, *bhajans*, and *kathās*—function as the bloodstream of civilization. They keep ethical values and spiritual insights supple and adaptable, preventing them from hardening into dogma. A story shared by a grandmother or sung by a wandering bard allows myth to remain current, personal, and relevant. In this way, oral tradition ensures that truth continues to breathe, generation after generation.

3. The Sacred Becoming Experiential

The culmination of living mythology is experience. When myth walks among people, it is no longer something to be believed or interpreted—it is something to be entered and lived. Rituals become thresholds between worlds, stories unfold as inner landscapes, and sacred sites turn into mirrors reflecting the seeker's own consciousness. Myth shifts from narration to participation.

Pilgrims do not merely hear of divine acts; they reenact them through movement, austerity, and immersion. A dip in the river echoes primordial purification, while a lamp lit at dusk recalls the first stirring of cosmic light. In these moments, participants cease to be observers of tradition and become its living carriers, embodying what was once only remembered.

This chapter reveals that mythology survives not because it is preserved in texts, but because it is lived in bodies, breath, and action. When the sacred becomes experiential, belief ripens into knowing, memory transforms into presence, and myth once again walks among people—quietly, unmistakably, shaped by human touch.

1. From Belief to Anubhava:

The ultimate aim of Vedic spirituality is not belief but *anubhava* —direct experience. Myth serves as the doorway; experience is the destination. The journey moves from reading about the divine to encountering it through *darśana*, the sacred seeing. When myth walks among people, the abstract idea of God becomes a tangible presence—encountered in a guru, a ritual moment, or a charged sacred space.

2. The Sanctification of the Ordinary:

As the sacred becomes experiential, the boundary between ritual and daily life dissolves. Ordinary actions are transfigured:

1. Eating becomes *prasāda*, a sanctified offering.
2. Walking becomes *parikrama*, a conscious circumambulation.
3. Work becomes *sevā*, selfless service.

The distinction between temple and marketplace fades, and the world itself becomes a field of dharma. In this transformation, mythology does not retreat into heaven or memory; it settles into life itself, where every act becomes a potential doorway to the sacred.

Summary: The Invitation

Chapter 17 affirms that we are not living in an age abandoned by myth; rather, myth awaits our invitation. Each act of selfless love, every moment of courage when truth is spoken against the odds, and every recognition of divinity in another human being reopens the doorway for the sacred to return. When lived with awareness, our lives themselves become the vessels through which ancient truths take new form. Myth does not need to be rediscovered—it needs to be embodied. When we choose dharma in daily life, the eternal once again learns to walk among people.

एकं सद् विप्रा बहुधा वदन्ति ।

सत्यप्रिया जनाः पश्यन्ति तं पथि चरन्तम् ॥

Ekaṁ Sad Viprā Bahudhā Vadanti

Satya-priyā Janāḥ Paśyanti Taṁ Pathi Carantam

Truth is one, though the wise speak of it in many ways.

Those who love Truth behold it walking openly among the people.

This is the final invitation of the chapter: not merely to believe in myth, but to live in such a way that the myth is compelled to return.

CHAPTER 18: THE RIVER AS GURU

In the Indian civilizational vision, a river is never merely a flow of water. It is a *guru—one* who teaches without words, corrects without punishment, and nourishes without demand. Chapter 18 turns to *Bharathapuzha* not as geography, but as wisdom embodied. She does not preach dharma; she demonstrates it. Like the great teachers of the epics, the river instructs through presence, patience, and perseverance, inviting humanity to relearn forgotten truths.

1. Bharathapuzha as Teacher

Bharathapuzha teaches as the greatest gurus do—through example. She flows without arrogance, bends without losing direction, and accepts without discrimination. Kings and mendicants, animals and children, saints and sinners—all are received equally at her banks. In this, she mirrors the wisdom of the *Bhagavad Gītā*, where Krishna teaches Arjuna that the highest wisdom is *samatva*—equanimity.

Like the Ganga descending from heaven through the matted locks of *Śiva*, *Bharathapuzha* reminds us that power must be tempered by humility. Her floods warn against excess; her droughts caution against neglect. When she recedes, she does not accuse—she reflects. In her silence during dry seasons lies a teaching more severe than any scripture: when dharma is forgotten, nourishment withdraws.

In the epics, rivers are conscious witnesses. The *Sarayu* listens as *Rama* departs *Ayodhya*. The *Yamuna* shelters *Krishna's* childhood. *Bharathapuzha*, too, has watched generations rise and fall and rituals flourish and fade. She teaches continuity—that while forms change, essence endures.

The chapter centers on the *Bharathapuzha* (also known as the *Nila*), a river that is the spiritual lifeline of Kerala. But the Nila here serves as an archetype for all sacred rivers—the Ganga, the Yamuna, and the Cauvery.

The River as a Witness:

Imagine standing on the sandy banks of the *Bharathapuzha* at twilight. This river has witnessed centuries of *Mamankam* festivals, heard the chanting of the *Vedas* from the banks of *Tirunavaya*, and received the ashes of countless ancestors.

1. The Lesson of Flow: The river teaches *pravaha*—the art of moving forward without clinging. It encounters rocks, dams, and drought, yet its nature is to seek the ocean. It teaches the spiritual aspirant that stagnation is death and movement is life.

2. The Lesson of Non-Discrimination: The river gives its water to the saint and the sinner alike. It does not judge the thirst of the tiger or the deer. It embodies the highest Vedantic truth of *Samadarshana* (equal vision).

2. Ecology as Dharma

In the *Mahābhārata, Bhīṣma* tells *Yudhiṣṭhira* that the protection of land, forests, waters, and creatures is *rājadharma*. To harm them is not merely environmental damage—it is moral failure. Chapter 18 reclaims this forgotten truth: ecology is not a modern concern; it is ancient dharma.

Bharathapuzha reveals this law vividly. When her banks are respected, she gives abundance. When her sands are plundered and her waters polluted, she responds not with anger, but with imbalance—erosion, scarcity, and silence. This is not punishment; it is a consequence. As the *Rāmāyaṇa* shows, when *Rāma* enters the forest, the forest protects him. When harmony exists, nature becomes an ally. When exploitation prevails, nature withdraws cooperation.

The river teaches *Ṛta*—cosmic order. Every intrusion disrupts a rhythm older than humanity. To live with the river is to live in alignment; to dominate it is to invite collapse. Thus, environmental responsibility is not activism alone—it is spiritual obedience to cosmic law.

The modern world speaks of "environmental protection." The Vedic world speaks of *Dharma*.

1. Rta (Cosmic Order):

In the *Rig Veda*, the universe is governed by *Rta*—the cosmic moral order. Nature follows this order instinctively; the sun rises, and the seasons change. Human beings are the only ones capable of violating *Rta*.

This chapter explains that polluting a river is not just a physical act; it is an ethical violation. It disrupts the cosmic harmony. To pollute water is to poison the blood of the Divine Mother (*Prakriti*).

2. Vasudhaiva Kutumbakam (The Earth is Family):

We often quote "the world is one family," but we limit "family" to humans. This chapter expands the definition. The trees, the river, the soil, and the animals are *kin*.

The Shift: We move from an "anthropocentric" view (man is the conqueror of nature) to a "theocentric" or "eco-centric" view (man is the servant/custodian of nature).

3. Ritual as Ecological Consciousness

In the Vedic worldview, ritual was never separate from ecology. A ritual was a contract with nature. When one offered water back to the river (*tarpana*), one acknowledged dependence. When one immersed oneself (*snāna*), one submitted ego to the larger flow. Rituals trained consciousness to see the river not as a resource, but as a relative—mother, teacher, witness.

The epics repeatedly show this intimacy. Before crossing rivers, heroes pray. Before battles, they offer water to ancestors. Even gods perform austerities on riverbanks. These acts were not symbolic gestures; they were ecological education encoded as sacred practice.

Chapter 18 reveals that ritual is memory in action. When rituals disappear, exploitation begins—not because people become evil, but because they forget relationships. To restore ritual is to restore reverence. When lamps are floated gently, when water is touched with mantra rather than machinery, the river is no longer an object—it is a presence.

Critics often dismiss rituals as superstitious waste. This chapter reinterprets ritual as a profound tool for ecological mindfulness.

1. The Logic of Sacredness:

When a Hindu performs a *Puja*, they start by invoking the holy rivers into the water pot (*Kalasha*) with the mantra. Here is the complete traditional Sanskrit mantra:

गङ्गे च यमुने चैव गोदावरि सरस्वति ।
नर्मदे सिन्धु कावेरी जलेऽस्मिन् सन्निधिं कुरु ॥

Gaṅge ca Yamune caiva Godāvari Sarasvatī |
Narmade Sindhu Kāverī jale'smin sannidhiṁ kuru ||

O Ganga, Yamuna, Godavari, Sarasvati,
Narmada, Sindhu, and Kaveri—
Please be present in this water.

A simple yet profound invocation, this mantra sacralises ordinary water by invoking the spiritual essence of India's sacred rivers. This mantra is commonly recited before bathing, invoking the sacred presence of all holy rivers in the water at hand.

Why do this?

1. *Re-enchantment:* It turns tap water into "sacred water. "You cannot carelessly waste or pollute what you consider sacred. Ritual forces the mind to pause and treat the element with reverence.
2. *Gratitude:* The ritual of *Sandhya vandanam* (twilight

worship) involves offering water back to the sun and the earth. It is a daily acknowledgment: "I take from nature, and I symbolically return to nature."

3. *The Bath as Purification:* A dip in the *Bharathapuzha* is not just to clean dirt from the skin (external), but to wash away *Malas* (impurities) of the mind (internal). When the river is seen as a purifier, the devotee is naturally compelled to keep the river pure.

The River as the Silent Guru

Unlike human teachers, the river never abandons the student. Even when ignored, polluted, or wounded, she continues to teach—through scarcity, through imbalance, through longing. *Bharathapuzha* stands as a *Mahāguru*, reminding humanity of its place within creation.

As the Upaniṣads teach, *Āchārya devo bhava*—the teacher is divine. In this chapter, the river herself becomes that teacher. To sit by her banks is to attend a timeless *gurukula*. To listen to her flow is to hear a lesson older than language.

The final teaching of Bharathapuzha is simple yet uncompromising: Protect what sustains you. Honour what teaches you. And remember—those who forget their guru forget themselves.

In learning again to bow to the river, humanity relearns how to stand rightly upon the earth.

The tragedy of the modern age is that the *Bharathapuzha*, like many rivers, is dying—choked by sand mining and waste. The chapter concludes with a haunting realization: when the river dies, the culture dies.

If the river is the guru, then seeing the river dry and polluted is seeing our teacher in distress. The spiritual imperative (*Dharma*) of our time is to heal the waters. We do not save the river for the river's sake; the river will eventually regenerate over geologic time. We save the river to save our own humanity. In *Bhagavad Gītā* 7.8, Lord Krishna gently reminds humanity that divinity is not distant or abstract—it flows quietly within the taste of water itself, revealing the sacred presence that sustains all life.

रसोऽहमप्सु कौन्तेय प्रभास्मि शशिसूर्ययोः ।
प्रणवः सर्ववेदेषु शब्दः खे पौरुषं नृषु ॥ **(*Bhagavad Gītā* 7.8)**

Raso'ham apsu Kaunteya prabhāsmi śaśi-sūryayoḥ |
Praṇavaḥ sarva-vedeṣu śabdaḥ khe pauruṣaṁ nṛṣu ||

O son of Kuntī, I am the taste in water;
I am the radiance in the moon and the sun.
I am the sacred syllable Om in all the Vedas,
the sound in space, and the vitality in human beings.

The Hymn to the Waters: Apah Suktam (Rig Veda 10.9)

The revered Ṛg Vedic mantras (Ṛg Veda 10.9.1–3) are traditionally chanted during water-centered rites, honouring water as a living sacred presence—bestower of healing, sustenance, purification, and inner illumination. The following verses are selected for daily contemplative practice:

1. The Invocation of Joy: The Sanskrit mantras:

आपो हि ष्ठा मयोभुवः ।
ता न ऊर्जे दधातन ।
महे रणाय चक्षसे ॥ (Ṛg Veda 10.9.1)

Apo hi stha mayobhuvah
Ta na urje dadhatana
Mahe ranaya chakshase

"O Waters, you are the source of happiness and delight.
Please grant us strength and nourishment (energy).
Grant us the vision to see the Great Truth (beautiful and auspicious)."

2. The Motherly Bond

यो वः शिवतमो रसः ।
तस्य भाजयतेह नः ।
उशतीरिव मातरः ॥ - (Ṛg Veda 10.9.2)

Yo vah shivatamo rasah

Tasya bhajayateha nah
Ushatiriva matarah

“O Waters, that most auspicious essence which is within you—
grant us a share of that here and now,
as loving mothers nourish their eager children.”

4. The Prayer for Healing

अप्सु मे सोमो अब्रवीद् ।
अन्तर्विश्वानि भेषजा ।
अग्निं च विश्वशम्भुवम् ॥ (Ṛg Veda 10.9.3)

Apsu me somo abravid
Antar vishvani bheshaja
Agnim cha vishva shambhuvam

"The Lord of the Moon (Soma) has told me that within the Waters
are all healing balms and cures (medicines).
And also within them is *Agni* (the digestive fire/energy) that blesses all."

How to Practice This (The "Water Moment")

You do not need to be a priest to perform this. You can integrate it into your daily life to shift from "consuming" water to "communing" with it.

1. Before Drinking: Hold your glass of water in both hands. Pause for three seconds. Look at the water and mentally recite the first verse (or simply: आपः प्राणाः, आपः औषधम् ॥ *Āpaḥ prāṇāḥ, āpaḥ auṣadham, "O Water, you are Life, you are Medicine"*). Visualise the water glowing with light before you drink it.

2. During the Shower: As the water touches your head (the *Sahasrara*), imagine it is the sacred Ganga or the *Bharathapuzha* washing away not just sweat but also fatigue, stress, and negativity (*Malas*).

3. Near a River: If you stand by a river, recite the second verse. See the river not as a resource to be exploited, but as a mother (*Matarah*) offering her milk to the earth.

By chanting this, you acknowledge that the water inside your body (which is 70% water) and the water in the river are one. That connection is the essence of *ecological dharma.*

PART VIII

THE DAKṢIṆA KUMBH A
New Spiritual Axis

CHAPTER 19: THE SOUTHERN KUMBH —CONTINUITY, NOT IMITATION

The return of Maha Magha in the South must not be read as a replication of the northern Kumbhas or as an echo seeking validation; it is continuity reasserting itself, not imitation asking permission. Sacred traditions do not copy forms—they reveal themselves when time ripens, and memory awakens. What surfaced on the banks of the *Bharathapuzha* was not a borrowed ritual but a remembered one, rising from beneath centuries of silence, rupture, and forgetting. The Southern Kumbh stands not as a mirror of Prayāga, Haridvāra, Ujjain, or Nāśik, but as their complement—a necessary counter-current within the sacred geography of *Bhāratavarṣa*, where North and South are not opposites but dialoguing poles of a single civilization. While the spiritual gaze has long turned northward, the Dakṣiṇa Kumbh restores balance by awakening a southern axis of sanctity, affirming that the cosmic Amṛuta fell here too, consecrating the "*Gaṅgā* of the South." To the untrained eye, this may appear as imitation; to the spiritual eye it is revelation —an expression of the one Truth manifesting according to its *kṣetra*. Just as fire burns differently in a forest, a sacrificial altar, or a humble lamp, the spirit of the Kumbh assumes the temperament of the land it touches. Here, Northern *jñāna* meets

Southern bhakti, ecological stewardship becomes sacred duty, and the river is restored not as a relic of the past but as a living, breathing source of grace.

1. Not Replication, but Revelation

True dharma does not imitate; it unfolds. It does not arrive by design or decree but emerges when remembrance, resolve, and inner readiness converge. The *Maha Magha* did not arise because someone set out to "create" a Kumbh in the South; it surfaced because a long-submerged current of consciousness found its way back to the light. Like a river that disappears underground and reappears centuries later, the tradition did not travel from elsewhere—it returned to itself.

In Vedic understanding, revelation (*pratyabhijñā*) carries a deeper authenticity than innovation. What appears in such sacred moments is not novelty, but recognition—*smṛti* awakening from dormancy. The rituals of Maha Magha—the river immersion, the lamps kindled at dusk, the vows undertaken in silence, the austerities embraced without announcement—bore the unmistakable weight of antiquity. Nothing needed to be staged, amplified, or advertised. The sacred recognized itself, and that recognition was enough.

Unlike the northern Kumbhas, shaped across centuries by royal patronage, imperial movement, and vast congregations, the Southern Kumbh carries a quieter signature. Its power lies not in proclamation but in presence, not in spectacle but in stillness. It does not declare its sanctity—it breathes it. This is not the replication of an outer form but the revelation of an inner essence.

There is a profound difference between a copy and a manifestation. Replication is mechanical—it is like carrying water from the Gaṅgā and pouring it into a constructed pool, where the form is present but the *prāṇa*, the living pulse, is absent. Revelation (*unmeṣa*), by contrast, is the patient act of digging into the local soil until one strikes the hidden spring that has always been there, waiting beneath layers of neglect and forgetfulness.

The spiritual logic of the Dakṣiṇa Kumbh rests on this truth: the sanctity of the *Bharathapuzha* (*Nīlā*) is *svayambhū*—self-existent. It does not borrow holiness from the North, nor does it require external validation. The river already carries within it the genetic memory of the Vedas once recited on its banks, of ancestral rites (*pitṛ-tarpaṇa*) performed for millennia, and of lives shaped in quiet intimacy with the sacred.

The Dakṣiṇa Kumbh, therefore, is an act of revelation—the lifting of the veil (*āvaraṇa*) of forgetfulness. Nothing new is being invented; a frequency long established by the Ṛṣis is simply being heard again. It is the realization that *Amṛuta*, the nectar of immortality, is not a geographical monopoly but a spiritual possibility—accessible wherever collective consciousness ripens into devotion, humility, and resolve. When that threshold is crossed, the sacred does not need to be summoned; it reveals itself.

2. Balance to the Northern Kumbhas

Civilizations remain inwardly healthy only when their sacred expressions are balanced across space, temperament, and mode of realization. When spirituality flows in a single direction—whether outward toward spectacle or inward toward silence—it loses harmony. The Kumbha tradition of Bhāratavarṣa was never meant to be monolithic; it was designed as a living system of complementary forces.

The northern Kumbhas are expansive, dramatic, and centrifugal in nature. They draw millions into visible convergence, turning geography into cosmology and time into theatre. These gatherings are vast enactments of myth, astronomy, and collective memory—cosmic assemblies where the many become one through scale, motion, and proclamation. Their power lies in visibility, momentum, and mass awakening.

The Southern Kumbh, by contrast, moves in a centripetal direction. It draws inward rather than outward, privileging absorption over assertion and depth over display. Where the North celebrates *mahā-saṅgama*—the grand coming together of multitudes—the South preserves *mauna-saṅgama*—silent communion, interior convergence, and unspoken recognition. Where the North foregrounds *Akhāḍās*, banners, and clearly defined spiritual orders, the South gives primacy to householder-sages, unnamed *tapasvīs*, temple lineages, and river-centered spirituality woven quietly into daily life.

This is not a hierarchy of forms but a polarity of functions—much like inhalation balancing exhalation or stillness completing movement. One without the other is incomplete. Without the Southern Kumbh, the civilizational rhythm remains unresolved; without a southern anchor, sacred energy risks drifting toward spectacle, mistaking scale for depth. Maha Magha restores gravitas, reminding the tradition that transformation does not always arrive in thunder. Sometimes it arrives as weight, silence, and inward settling.

The spiritual anatomy of Bharat has always required equilibrium. The North—home to the Himalayas, Kāśī, and Prayāga—represents ascending energy (*ūrdhva-retas*): renunciation, austerity, transcendence, and the vertical pull toward the Absolute. It is the realm of Śiva, of upward striving, of fire rising toward the sky.

The South embodies descending grace—the realm of *Śakti*, preservation, nourishment, and continuity. Here, the sacred does not soar away from life; it enters it, stabilizes it, and sustains it. Grace flows downward into form, relationship, and ecology.

This balance is illuminated in the ancient myth of Sage Agastya. When the gods and sages assembled in the Himalayas for the divine wedding of Śiva and Pārvatī, the earth tilted dangerously northward under the sheer weight of sanctity. To restore cosmic balance, Śiva commanded Agastya to journey south. Agastya's presence in the Dakṣiṇa was not exile but necessity. By settling in the South, he equalized the spiritual mass of the world and made the land fit again to receive grace.

In the modern imagination, however, the spiritual centre of gravity has once more tilted overwhelmingly toward the North. Sacred journeys, pilgrim narratives, and popular memory often overlook the southern axis of power and preservation. The Dakṣiṇa Kumbh functions today as the Agastya Principle reborn. It restores energetic equilibrium, reminding the nation that India's spiritual circuit is incomplete unless consciousness flows from the Himalayas to the Ocean—and returns again.

The Maha Magha does not compete with the northern Kumbhas; it completes them. Together, they form a single mandala of movement and stillness, ascent and descent, fire and water—ensuring that the sacred life of the civilization remains whole, grounded, and alive.

3. Kerala's Sacred Temperament

Kerala does not *receive* the sacred as an arrival from elsewhere; it *hosts* it as a natural condition of the land. Sanctity here is not imposed, announced, or amplified—it is absorbed. The spiritual temperament of Kerala has been shaped over centuries by water and rain, fertility and restraint, rhythm and continuity. This is a land where abundance does not produce excess, and devotion does not seek display.

The rivers of Kerala are not conquerors carving their authority into stone; they are companions, flowing intimately through villages, temples, rice fields, and daily lives. The Bharathapuzha does not dominate the land—it educates it. It teaches patience through its seasonal flow, humility through its widening banks, and memory through its silent endurance. Life here is organized *with* water, not against it.

Kerala's spirituality has never been about the conquest of nature but about sustained conversation with it. Temples open inward rather than upward, inviting the devotee into stillness rather than awe. Rituals emphasize rhythm over rhetoric and repetition over revelation. Saints of this land rarely gathered crowds; they sought clarity. Their power lay in presence, not proclamation. This temperament makes Kerala uniquely receptive to a Kumbh that values substance over size, depth over density.

Maha Magha, therefore, does not feel imported into Kerala; it feels inevitable. The people arrive without frenzy. The rituals unfold without excess. The river receives without drama. There is no sense of invasion—only recognition. This is Kerala's genius: sacred without strain, devotion without display. The Southern Kumbh belongs here because the land itself understands continuity better than conquest.

If the northern Kumbh is a roaring fire that awakens through blaze and heat, the Southern Kumbh is a steady oil lamp—*nilavilakku*—glowing quietly, illuminating without consuming. Both are sacred, but they speak different languages of the same truth.

Every land possesses a *svabhāva*—an inherent spiritual temperament. Kerala's ethos is distinct, and the Dakṣiṇa Kumbh naturally reflects it.

1. *Tantra over Tamasha:*

While northern gatherings often express ecstatic intensity and raw spiritual energy, Kerala's tradition is deeply rooted in *Tantra Śāstra*—precision, cleanliness, order, and inward alignment. Worship here is disciplined and exacting, guided by timing, geometry, and breath. The Southern Kumbh does not rise through noise; it resonates through *Nāda*—subtle sound, inner vibration, and harmonic presence.

2. Simplicity as Aesthetic:

Kerala's visual language is restrained and eloquent: the white *mundu* symbolizing purity and equality, the bronze lamp holding inner light, and the absence of garish ornamentation. The festival does not overwhelm the landscape; it bows to it. Greenery is not decorated—it is honoured. Space is left open so silence may speak.

3. Nature as Deity:

In Kerala, the *kāvu*—the sacred grove—is as revered as the temple sanctum. Trees, serpents, rivers, and soil are not symbols of the divine; they are its immediate expressions. The Dakṣiṇa Kumbh therefore, carries an inherently ecological consciousness. It does not seek to conquer the river; it submits to it. The highest *prasāda* offered here is not food or token—it is a clean riverbank, an unpolluted flow, and a restored relationship between human life and natural order. In this land, the sacred is not staged. It is lived. And because of this, the Southern Kumbh does not appear as an event—it unfolds as a continuation of what Kerala has always known.

4. Tantra as the Hidden Architecture of the Dakṣiṇa Kumbh:

The Southern Kumbh is sustained not by spectacle, but by Tantra—the silent architecture that aligns body, land, time, and element. Beneath Maha Magha flows a living Tantric intelligence where truth is not invented but remembered (*pratyabhijñā*). The Bharathapuzha awakens its own latent *śakti* when readiness converges, revealing sanctity rather than borrowing it. Balancing the expansive, ascending energy of the northern Kumbhas, the Dakṣiṇa Kumbh expresses descending grace—containment, depth, and inward absorption—echoing the Agastya principle of civilizational equilibrium. Rooted in Kerala's meticulous Tantric ecology, where lamp, temple, river, and silence are conscious instruments, ritual becomes ecological dharma. Here, care is worship, preservation is offering, and restraint is power. The Southern Kumbh thus shows that continuity outweighs novelty: a river can be a guru, silence can be initiation, and Tantra—quietly—restores balance by revealing what was always present.

4. The Southern Kumbh as Civilizational Memory

The Southern Kumbh reminds *Bhārata* of a truth often forgotten in ages of imitation and haste: sacred traditions do not endure by being reproduced everywhere, but by being remembered where they belong. Maha Magha does not seek to rival the northern Kumbhas, nor does it attempt to mirror their scale or spectacle. It completes them. Where the North ascends, the South grounds; where the North proclaims, the South absorbs. Together, they form a complete civilizational rhythm, affirming that sacred geography is not linear or centralized but circular, distributed, and layered across the land.

In this light, the Southern Kumbh is not a novelty introduced into history, but a forgotten footnote rediscovered—now read aloud by time itself. It restores depth to memory, reminding the nation that the sacred does not always announce itself with thunder; sometimes it returns as quiet recognition. The South, in welcoming Maha Magha, does not imitate the North—it remembers its own inheritance, long carried in rivers, rituals, and restraint.

The *Dakṣiṇa Kumbh* offers something the modern world is starved of spiritual ecology. It invites the seeker not merely to witness a gathering but to enter a *sādhanā*—one that fuses the ancient Vedic fire of remembrance with the cool, green wisdom of the South. Here, devotion is inseparable from care, ritual from responsibility, and sanctity from sustainability. This is the silent current that completes the circle of Dharma, ensuring that tradition remains alive not through repetition, but through right placement.

As the oil fills the lamp, as the river fills the ocean,

So may Grace fill the South—and through it, the whole of Bhārata.

CHAPTER 20: THE FUTURE FLOW

Where Memory Becomes Movement

Every sacred return leaves behind a question that time alone will answer: will this remain a moment, or will it become a current? The re-emergence of *Maha Magha* is not meant to close with the final ritual or the dispersal of pilgrims; it is meant to inaugurate continuity. A river does not exist for a single flood or spectacle —it exists to flow, sometimes visible, sometimes hidden, always faithful to its source. This chapter turns its gaze forward, not merely across years, but across cycles of consciousness, asking how the rediscovered sanctity of the South may be protected, deepened, and transmitted without hardening into ritual excess or dissolving into collective amnesia.

The future of *Maha Magha* does not lie in scale alone, but in right repetition—a return that refines rather than replicates, deepens rather than amplifies. Each reappearance must carry greater clarity, restraint, and inner alignment, allowing the essence to mature rather than the form to inflate. In this way, Maha Magha resists becoming an event that seeks attention and instead becomes a discipline that shapes character, ecology, and collective memory.

Like the river it honors, the *Dakṣiṇa Kumbh* does not cease when it slips beneath the surface. It may change course, it may flow unseen, but its movement is unbroken. This chapter therefore marks not an ending, but a *saṅkalpa*—a solemn vow to carry the current forward through daily conduct, ecological responsibility, ritual integrity, and intergenerational transmission. It shifts the focus from the exhilaration of gathering to the quieter, more demanding work of civilization-building.

We are not merely preparing for another return; we are cultivating a living inheritance. What is planted here is not a festival, but a forest—one whose shade will shelter generations we will never meet, and whose roots will draw nourishment from a memory older than time itself.

1. The Twelve-Year Vision: Time as a Sacred Spiral

1. The Mandala of Return

In Indic cosmology, twelve years is not an arbitrary measure of time; it is a complete breath of becoming. It is the period of *Brihaspati's* (Jupiter's) revolution—the governor of wisdom, expansion, and karmic ripening. What this cycle marks is not repetition but maturation: the slow alchemy by which intention becomes character and memory becomes culture. The Northern Kumbhas align themselves to this rhythm not as a human schedule, but as a listening to cosmic timing. The *Dakṣiṇa Kumbh*, too, must be envisioned within this sacred spiral—not as a calendar obligation, but as a conscious re-entry into time itself.

Each twelve-year return of Maha Magha is therefore not a reenactment of form, but a deepening of resolve. The vision ahead is not "larger," but truer; not louder, but clearer. Cleaner riverbanks, fewer distractions, greater silence, and deeper *sādhanā* must replace the modern impulse toward spectacle. The future flow demands fidelity to essence rather than attraction to scale, restraint rather than excess, and presence rather than performance.

Between these twelve-year thresholds, the river itself becomes the primary custodian of memory. Annual observances, seasonal rites, and sustained ecological guardianship ensure that sanctity is not compressed into a single moment but diffused into everyday life. When Maha Magha returns, it should not arrive as a stranger summoned by announcement, but as a long-awaited guest welcomed by recognition. The question is not when Maha Magha returns, but whether the land, the water, and the people are inwardly prepared to receive it once more.

In the Vedic understanding, time is cyclical and pedagogical. A *Maha Kumbh* occurs every twelve years because this is the time required for a generation to mature, for a seed to become a fruit-bearing tree, and for an idea to descend from philosophy into habit. What is entrusted to this cycle is not mere continuity but transformation.

2. The Ecological Vow: Regeneration as Ritual:

The twelve-year vision ahead is not only spiritual; it is regenerative. Dharma, when fully lived, must restore what it touches. Thus, the future of Maha Magha binds ritual to responsibility and sanctity to stewardship.

***Years 1–4: Cleansing (Śuddhi)*:**

The *first phase* is an act of repentance and repair. The physical removal of plastic, debris, and pollutants from the *Nila* becomes the foundational rite. The meaning of the "*Holy Dip*" is consciously redefined: before one immerses the body in sacred water, one must cleanse the water itself. Purification begins not downstream, but inward.

Years 5–8: Greening (Prāṇa):

The *second phase* restores breath to the riverbanks. *Nakṣatra*

Vanams—groves aligned with stellar wisdom—are planted along the shores, re-weaving cosmic order into terrestrial life. Shade returns. Birds return. The riverbanks begin to breathe again, not as manicured grounds, but as living ecologies.

Years 9–12: Flowing (Dharā-Pravāha):

The *final phase* attends to the river's unseen body. Small check dams, revived aquifers, and traditional water-holding structures restore the natural rhythm of flow. The river is allowed to remember how to hold, release, and sustain itself.

By the time the next *Maha Magha* arrives, the pilgrim should witness not merely a festival but a resurrected river—a living testament to Vedic ecology in practice. The twelve-year vision is thus to transform the *Bharathapuzha* into a living laboratory of *dharmic* renewal, where time, water, and consciousness move together in harmony.

This is the sacred spiral of return: not a circle that repeats, but a mandala that deepens.

2. The Triad of Dharma Guardians: Youth, Scholars, Institutions

Continuity as Transmission

A civilization does not endure by stone and spectacle, but by transmission. Monuments may mark memory, but only living lineages carry it forward. The future of *Maha Magha* cannot rest upon organizers or calendars alone; it must be stewarded by three conscious forces—three living pillars through which continuity breathes: Youth, Scholars, and Institutions. Together, they form a tripod of balance. Remove one, and the flame flickers. Align all three, and the sacred current becomes self-sustaining.

A. The Youth: Flame-Bearers, Not Spectators:

1. The Hands of the River: Memory to Might:

The youth are not meant to inherit Maha Magha as nostalgia; they are meant to inherit it as responsibility. Their role is not crowd-building but meaning-holding. When the young are reduced to spectators, tradition becomes performance. When they are invited into discipline, tradition becomes bloodstream.

In this vision, the youth emerge as *Dharma Rakṣakas* of the present, not the future. They move from screens to streams, from consumption to custodianship. They become river guardians, ritual learners, oral historians, and ecological sentinels. When young hands clean the river after ritual, when young voices chant without amplification, when young feet walk pilgrim paths with restraint, Maha Magha moves from memory into muscle.

The flame is never passed by instruction alone; it is passed by participation. We envision the rise of *River Warriors*—young men and women trained not only in Vedic recitation but also in water literacy, traditional hydrology, organic farming, and ecological ethics. They are the ones who will take ancient myths and retell them in the digital language of the twenty-first century, not to trivialise them, but to make the Nila present in the global consciousness. In their hands, tradition does not retreat from modernity; it re-enters it with dignity.

B. The Scholars: Interpreters of Depth:

2. The Eyes of Wisdom:

Passion without knowledge can become distorted. Ritual without understanding can harden into habit. Scholars serve as the eyes of the movement, ensuring that depth is not lost to enthusiasm. Their role is not to fossilize Maha Magha into archives but to interpret its grammar—Vedic, Tantric, ecological, historical, and civilizational. They stand as bridges between lived ritual and reflective understanding. Through careful research, translation, and contextual explanation, they keep meaning accessible without making it shallow.

Scholarship here is seva, not authority. Scholars are called to rediscover lost *tīrthas* along the river, to map forgotten ritual geographies, and to translate *Sanskrit* and *Malayalam* manuscripts that hold the layered memory of the *Nila*. They ensure that *the Dakṣiṇa Kumbh* remains rooted in *śāstra* and lived tradition, preventing it from dissolving into a spectacle of tourism or a diluted cultural brand. Their presence anchors enthusiasm to wisdom, ensuring that revival remains authentic rather than performative.

C. The Institutions: Custodians, Not Controllers:

3. The Spine of Structure:

Spiritual vitality without structure risks chaos; structure without humility risks domination. Institutions exist to provide the spine, not the spotlight. Temples, āśrams, educational bodies, Devastanams, cultural trusts, and modern ecological organizations must function as protective vessels rather than proprietors. Their task is to safeguard ritual purity, regulate excess, enforce ecological responsibility, and resist commercialisation. Institutions succeed precisely when they make themselves increasingly invisible, allowing the river, the ritual, and the seeker to remain central. When institutions serve the sacred rather than manage it, continuity becomes effortless.

This vision also marks the quiet end of sectarianism. *Śaivites* and *Vaiṣṇavites*, *Tantrics* and *Vedāntins*, scholars and environmentalists must learn to sit at the same table. Along the banks of the Nila, the river itself becomes the unifying deity

—the visible body of Dharma demanding care, restraint, and reverence.

D. The Living Tripod of Continuity:

4. How a Sacred Return Becomes a Civilizational Flow

For a sacred tradition to endure, it must rest upon forces that are alive, balanced, and mutually supportive. Fire alone cannot travel; it requires hands to carry it, eyes to guide it, and a body to bear its weight. In the same way, the flame of *Maha Magha*—rekindled after centuries—cannot survive the unpredictable winds of modernity without a stable foundation. That foundation is the Living Tripod of Continuity: Youth, Scholars, and Institutions.

This tripod does not enforce continuity through rules or authority. It allows continuity to arise naturally—through participation, understanding, and protection. When these three stand aligned, tradition ceases to be fragile. It becomes resilient, adaptive, and self-renewing—like the river that reshapes its banks without losing its source.

5. Youth: The Hands That Serve and Carry:

Embodiment Before Explanation

The youth represent the kinetic energy of continuity. They are the hands through which tradition is lifted from memory into action. Without them, Maha Magha risks becoming an archive; with them, it becomes a lived experience.

Their role is not to replicate rituals mechanically, but to embody restraint, discipline, and reverence in action. When young hands clean the river before entering it, when they learn chants by listening rather than recording, and when they walk pilgrim paths instead of driving past them, they internalize values that no sermon can transmit. Through the body, the tradition enters the soul.

In this way, the youth do not merely "participate" in Maha Magha—they become its carriers. They learn that service is not auxiliary to ritual; it *is* ritual. Their engagement transforms the Kumbh from an occasional gathering into a generational inheritance. The flame passes naturally because it has been felt, not just described.

6. Scholars: The Eyes That See and Interpret:

Meaning as Protection

If youth are the hands of continuity, scholars are its eyes. They ensure that what is carried is not distorted, diluted, or misunderstood. In an age of rapid information and shallow interpretation, scholarship becomes a form of spiritual protection.

The task of scholars is not to dominate the tradition with theory but to clarify its inner grammar—the Vedic foundations, Tantric precision, ecological intelligence, and historical context that give Maha Magha its coherence. They help distinguish essence from embellishment, discipline from display, and continuity from imitation.

Through research, translation, and contextual teaching, scholars keep the ritual intelligible without reducing it to explanation alone. They illuminate why silence matters, why scale is restrained, and why water is treated as a witness rather than a resource. Their work ensures that Maha Magha does not collapse into spectacle or become vulnerable to ideological misuse.

In this sense, scholarship is not authority—it is seva through understanding, guarding the depth that allows the tradition to evolve without losing its centre.

7. Institutions: The Spine That Supports Without Controlling:

Structure in Service of the Sacred

Every living body requires a spine—firm enough to hold form, flexible enough to allow movement. Institutions serve this role in the continuity of Maha Magha. They provide structure without suffocation, support without ownership.

Temples, āśrams, Devastanams, cultural bodies, and ecological organizations are not meant to claim the sacred; they are meant to protect its conditions. Their responsibility lies in maintaining ritual purity, regulating excess, ensuring ecological compliance, and shielding the tradition from commercialization and political appropriation.

The highest success of an institution is not visibility but invisibility. When governance is quiet, when regulation is ethical, and when stewardship is rooted in humility, the seeker remains at the center. Institutions become vessels through which the sacred flows, not gates that restrict it. By standing together—across sects, disciplines, and ideologies—institutions also dissolve fragmentation. The river becomes the common altar. Dharma becomes the shared language.

8. Alignment: When Continuity Becomes Effortless:

When hands, eyes, and spine move in harmony, continuity no longer requires enforcement. It becomes organic, like breath. The youth carry with devotion, scholars guide with clarity, and institutions protect with restraint. No single pillar dominates; each complements the others.

This is how Maha Magha evolves from a restored event into a civilizational current. It no longer depends on announcements or anniversaries. It lives in habits, landscapes, and inner orientations. The Kumbh becomes not something one attends, but something one *belongs to*. In this alignment, Maha Magha ceases to be a festival on the river. It becomes the river flowing through civilization itself.

3. Carrying the Flame Forward

1. From Event to Embodied Dharma

The ultimate question the future will ask is disarmingly simple: What remains when the lamps are extinguished, and the crowds disperse? If *Maha Magha* is true, its proof will not be found in photographs or attendance numbers, but in the habits, it leaves behind.

A genuine sacred return does not end with ritual completion; it continues as transformed conduct. The river must remain cleaner long after the final dip. Devotion must grow quieter, not louder. Personal *sādhanā* must deepen beyond public visibility. Ecology must cease to be a campaign and return to its rightful place—as worship practiced without announcement.

Carrying the flame forward does not mean recreating the event. It means living its intelligence daily. Every mindful entry into water, every act of restraint chosen over convenience, every ancestor remembered without display, and every lamp lit at dusk without witnesses becomes a continuation of Maha Magha. In this way, the Kumbh moves from the riverbank into the bloodstream of life. The future flow is therefore not outward in scale—it is inward in depth and onward in time.

2. Agni Paramparā: The Fire That Is Never Extinguished:

In the Vedic tradition, sacred fire is never put out. When a *yajña* concludes, the flame is carefully transferred to another vessel. This unbroken succession—*Agni Paramparā*—ensures that the fire lives beyond the ritual.

The Dakṣiṇa Kumbh is such a flame. A lamp has been lit in the South—not to blaze briefly, but to burn steadily across generations. When pilgrims depart, the responsibility does not dissolve; it relocates. The fire must now be carried in conduct, memory, and restraint.

To guard this flame is not a collective project alone—it is an individual vow. Each household that protects water, each child taught reverence before explanation, and each silence honoured as sacred becomes a new vessel for the same fire.

The Internal Kumbh: Where the River Truly Meets:

The chapter reminds us that the deepest pilgrimage does not occur on land. The ultimate river flows within—the *Suṣumṇā Nāḍī*, the central channel of consciousness. The ultimate Kumbh is not a confluence of rivers, but the union of the soul with the Divine.

External ritual prepares the body. Internal *sādhanā* completes the journey. Maha Magha points the seeker inward, toward that silent meeting where effort dissolves into grace. When the outer Kumbh awakens the inner one, the ritual has fulfilled its highest purpose.

Thus, the future of Maha Magha is not dependent on geography alone. It survives wherever inner alignment is preserved.

Transmission: The Gesture That Outlives Words:

Imagine an elder standing in the waters of the *Bharathapuzha*, lifting a copper pot filled from the river, and placing it gently into the hands of a child. No instruction is given. No oath is spoken. Yet everything is transmitted. The gesture says, "I *have kept the river alive for you. Now, you must keep it alive for those who will come after."* This is how Dharma moves forward—not through command, but through trust. Not through repetition, but through responsibility.

The River Continues:

Maha Magha has returned—but it does not end here. Like the *Bharathapuzha* itself, its destiny is to flow sometimes visible, sometimes subterranean, always faithful to its source.

If guarded with humility and carried with care, the Southern Kumbh will not fade again into silence. It will wait. It will remember. And when time ripens once more, it will rise—not as spectacle, but as truth reclaimed.

The future of Maha Magha is not something we plan. It is something we become.

Final Invocation: Trusting the Current

The Future Flow is an invitation to trust the river.
The work has begun.
The seeds are sown.
The ancestors are watching.

ॐ पूर्णमदः पूर्णमिदं
पूर्णात् पूर्णमुदच्यते ।
पूर्णस्य पूर्णमादाय
पूर्णमेवावशिष्यते ॥

"Om Pūrṇamadaḥ Pūrṇamidam

Pūrṇāt Pūrṇamudacyate

Pūrṇasya Pūrṇamādāya

Pūrṇamevāvaśiṣyate."

That is infinite. This is infinite.

From the infinite, the infinite proceeds.

Yet, the infinite remains.

PART IX

CIVILISATIONAL SIGNIFICANCE
Beyond Festival, Toward Memory

CHAPTER 21: MAHA MAGHA — KERALA'S SACRED RETURN TO INDIA'S CIVILISATIONAL MAP

Kerala's Civilizations are not sustained by monuments alone, nor remembered solely through dynasties and economies. They endure through ritual memory—through the moments when human life consciously aligns itself with cosmic time. In the Bharatiya civilizational vision, festivals are not seasonal celebrations; they are temporal gateways through which society periodically re-enters sacred order.

Maha Magha stands among these rare civilizational gateways. Its revival in Kerala is not an innovation, nor a regional assertion seeking validation. It is a remembering—a reawakening of Kerala's ancient position within the pan-Indian sacred geography. Through Maha Magha, Kerala does not place itself alongside the great *tīrthas* of India; it returns to where it has always belonged.

1. Sacred Geography: How India Remembers Itself

India has never known itself primarily through political

borders. Its true map is drawn through tīrthas, rivers, mountains, and calendrical alignments. This sacred cartography binds distant regions into a single civilizational body.

Kashi gathers time through death and liberation.
Prayaga gathers rivers and eras.
Ujjain aligns the cosmos through *Mahākāla*.
Haridwar and Nashik mark the descent and ascent of the sacred flow.

Each of these centres reaffirms its civilizational role through periodic convergence aligned with planetary time, especially the twelve-year cycle of Brihaspati (Jupiter).

Maha Magha performs this same function for Kerala. By synchronizing the ritual life of the *Bharathapuzha* with the *Magha nakshatra* and the Jovian cycle, Kerala declares—not rhetorically, but ritually—that it participates in the same cosmic grammar that governs the Kumbh traditions of the rest of *Bharatavarsha*. This is not imitation. It is structural continuity. Sacred time recognizes no periphery.

2. Mamankam and Maha Magha: Two Names, One Sacred Pulse

Kerala's place on the pan-Indian sacred map has historically been marked by Mamankam, celebrated on the banks of the River Nila at Tirunavaya. Linguistically, ritually, and astrologically, Mamankam is the regional evolution of *Maha Magha*. The sacred map of the South is not divided by language or coastlines but united by the twelve-year Jovian rhythm:

1. In Kumbakonam, when Jupiter enters *Simha Rāśi* and the Moon resides in Magha, *Mahāmaham* is observed on the banks of the Kaveri—rightly known as the "Kumbh of the South."

2. In Tirunavaya, this same alignment historically summoned Mamankam on the banks of the Bharathapuzha.

These are not parallel inventions. They are twin nodes of the same sacred circuit—one on the eastern flow of the Kaveri, the other on the western course of the Nila. Together, they complete the southern arc of the pan-Indian Maha Magha field. In reclaiming Maha Magha, Kerala is not borrowing sanctity; it is reclaiming its original rhythm.

3. Bharathapuzha: From Regional River to Civilizational Witness

Rivers become sacred not by decree, but by participation in sacred time. During Maha Magha, the Bharathapuzha—revered as the Nila—transcends its regional identity. It becomes a national tīrtha, a southern witness to the same civilizational vow undertaken at Ganga, Kaveri, and Godavari.

Puranic memory speaks of *Gaṅgā-sannidhya*—the presence of all sacred rivers during auspicious cosmic alignments. In this vision, rivers are not static channels but living deities, periodically gathering to cleanse not only humanity but also themselves.

Kerala's role in this sacred ecology is profound. The Sahyadri ranges, from which the Nila arises, are envisioned as a purificatory womb—the rain-bearing, life-renewing source that feeds the sanctity of the South. Maha Magha thus positions Kerala not as a receiver alone, but as a custodian of sacred replenishment. The river becomes not a resource, but a participant in Dharma.

4. Tirunavaya: The Prayaga of the West

Every sacred map requires anchoring points. On Kerala's sacred map, Tirunavaya emerges as the western counterpart to Prayaga. Anchored by the *Navamukunda* Temple, this confluence of river, ritual, and time becomes the locus where cosmic alignment touches lived history.

Here, Maha Magha does not merely sanctify water—it sanctifies memory. The belief that the Nila attains Ganga-like potency during this period is not metaphorical; it is civilizational shorthand for a deeper truth: when time aligns, geography transforms. Through Tirunavaya, Kerala is inscribed onto the same sacred parchment that holds Kashi and Prayaga.

5. From Sacred Convergence to Historical Distortion

Kerala's story carries a unique divergence. While Mahāmaham at Kumbakonam retained a largely spiritual character, Mamankam in Kerala gradually absorbed martial and political dimensions. Power struggles, the chaver warriors, and royal assertions came to dominate collective memory. Yet beneath this historical turbulence, the sacred clock never stopped ticking.

Maha Magha did not disappear—it was overlaid. The present rejuvenation of Maha Magha is therefore not an invention, nor a correction of history, but a restoration of depth—a return from surface narratives to underlying sacred time. It recenters Kerala's identity from spectacle back to spiritual alignment.

6. Beyond Religion: A Civilizational Declaration

Maha Magha is not sectarian. It belongs neither to a single temple nor to institutional authority. Its true sovereignty lies in its ecological, temporal, and ethical vision. It affirms that:

1. Rivers are ancestors, not utilities.

2. Ecology is worship, not activism.

3. Time is sacred, not consumable.

In an age where culture risks becoming performance and

heritage a commodity, Maha Magha stands as a quiet act of civilizational self-respect.

Conclusion: When Kerala Remembers, India Responds

Sacred maps are redrawn not by force, but by remembrance. With the return of Maha Magha, Kerala steps once more into pan-Indian sacred time—not as an echo, but as a western anchor of the southern Kumbh tradition. The Nila flows again not only through geography but also through civilizational consciousness.

A civilization survives not by preserving stone,
but by remembering when to gather,
where to bathe,
and how to bow before Time.

Here, the river remembers the nation.
Here, the South remembers its vow.
Here, Kerala's Kumbh quietly returns home.

GLOSSARY

Vedic Principles and Cosmic Order

1. **Agni** – The Vedic fire deity, a living mediator between humans and the divine; the eternal witness (*sākṣī*) to vows, rituals, and memory.
2. **Agni-sākṣi** – Fire as witness; testifying to actions, transitions, and restorations beyond social or legal acknowledgment.
3. **Ātman** – The innermost Self, revealed when ego and limitation are transcended; the flame of the Nilavilakku symbolizes this unveiling.
4. **Buddhi** – Discriminative intellect; like the wick of the Nilavilakku, upright, refined, and sustaining illumination under the guidance of devotion.
5. **Ṛta** – Primordial cosmic order governing natural cycles, truth, and moral harmony; the foundation of dharma and sacred time.
6. **Dharma** – Righteous duty and cosmic law, sustaining order between the universe, society, and individual life.

Divine Beings and Avatāras

7. **Avatāra** – A divine descent; an incarnation of the Supreme (especially Vishnu) to restore dharma.
8. **Parashurāma** – The sixth avatāra of Vishnu, bearer of the

axe, linked with reclaiming and consecrating Kerala.

9. **Vishnu** – The Preserver; sustaining cosmic balance and guiding sacred time.
10. **Brahmā** – The Creator in the Trimūrti, associated with emergence and continuity.
11. **Śiva (Nīlakaṇṭha / Īśvara)** – The dissolving principle; ascetic consciousness absorbing Hālāhala to protect creation.
12. **Devas** – Cosmic intelligences upholding ṛta; maintain universal order and witness sacred cycles.
13. **Asuras** – Beings of unrefined power and instinct; essential participants in transformation, representing light and shadow.
14. **Mohini** – Vishnu's enchanting form, safeguarding Amṛta and balancing cosmic forces.

Sacred Time, Space, and Alignment

15. **Kala / Kāla (Sacred Time)** – Time as qualitative, alive, and transformative; flows differently in sacred alignments.
16. **Sacred Time** – Time experienced as renewal rather than linear succession, allowing re-entry into cosmic rhythm.
17. **Magha Māsa** – The annual lunar month dedicated to purification, dharmic living, and karmic renewal.
18. **Maha Magha** – A rare convergence where time, space, and consciousness align; sacred time becomes lived experience.
19. **Uttarāyaṇa** – The Sun's northward journey, associated with spiritual ascent, illumination, and auspiciousness.
20. **Triadic Alignment** – Simultaneous harmony of kāla

(time), deśa (space), and cetanā (consciousness); defines Maha Magha.

21. **Sacred Space (Deśa)** – Geography infused with memory, consciousness, and capacity for spiritual transformation.

22. **Tīrtha** – Sacred crossing points where human intention, geography, and divine realms intersect; rivers and confluences are enduring tīrthas.

23. **Nakṣatra (Magha)** – Lunar constellation associated with ancestry, authority, and karmic continuity.

Rituals, Practices, and Disciplines

24. **Yajña / Yāga** – Sacred offering; a cosmic act of participation.

25. **Pancha Mahā Yajñas** – Five daily sacrifices: Deva, Pitṛ, Bhūta, Manuṣya, Ṛṣi Yajñas, sustaining cosmic and social harmony.

26. **Snāna / Magha Snāna / Holy Dip** – Ritual immersion symbolizing purification, re-entry into cosmic memory, and alignment with sacred time.

27. **Pūjā** – Ritual worship establishing reciprocal alignment between human and divine.

28. **Saṁskāra** – Rituals marking life stages, forming karmic impressions, and linking individual existence with cosmic rhythm.

29. **Tapas / Tapas-Anuśāsana** – Spiritual discipline and restraint; inner heat that purifies consciousness and consecrates place.

30. **Sādhanā** – Spiritual practice cultivating internal transformation beyond public ritual.

31. **Saṅkalpa** – Conscious, sustained resolve; transforms intention into sacred force.

32. **Dāna** – Sacred giving, restoring balance and aligning human action with dharma.

33. **Pitṛ-kārya / Pitṛ Yajña** – Ritual duties for ancestors, ensuring karmic continuity, reconciliation, and remembrance.

34. **Piṇḍa Dāna** – Offering of food to ancestors, sustaining lineage and memory.

35. **Tarpana** – Water offerings to ancestors; "to satiate" and release karmic bonds.

36. **Svadhā** – Utterance in ancestor rites meaning "may this be received"; affirms nourishment and peace.

Rivers, Geography, and Sacred Sites

37. **Bhūmi** – Sacred land; living and consecrated presence beyond physical territory.

38. **Bharathapuzha (Nila / Dakṣiṇa Gaṅgā)** – Kerala's sacred river; carrier of memory, culture, and spiritual continuity.

39. **Kṣetra** – Sacred field or domain imbued with divine energy.

40. **Navayoga Kṣetra** – Site where nine yogic paths converge, enabling spiritual union.

41. **Trimūrti Saṅgamam / Sañcāra** – Convergence of creation, preservation, and dissolution principles; rivers and confluences manifest this alignment.

42. **Utsava** – Communal festivals aligning social life with cosmic rhythm.

43. **Nakṣatra Vanams** – Star-aligned groves along riverbanks integrating cosmic order into ecology.

Mythology and Cosmic Narratives

44. **Samudra Manthana** – Churning of the cosmic ocean; metaphor for transformation, balancing chaos and order to yield immortality (*Amṛta*).
45. **Amṛta** – Nectar of immortality; symbolizes timeless consciousness.
46. **Hālāhala** – Primordial poison; represents karmic toxicity and suffering to be transformed.
47. **Mandara Parvata** – Cosmic mountain used as the churning rod; axis of transformation.
48. **Vasuki** – Divine serpent used as churning rope; represents latent energy and *prāṇa*.
49. **Kalaśa / Kumbh** – Sacred vessels; containers of Amṛta and convergence of space, time, and human participation.
50. **Magha Nakṣatra / Makara Saṅkrānti** – Lunar and solar events that activate ancestral and cosmic alignments.

Civilizational Concepts and Maha Magha Philosophy

51. **Akhāḍā** – Disciplined collective of practitioners; living ethos of shared dharmic resolve.
52. **Anusmṛti (Civilizational Remembering)** – Conscious revival of dormant traditions, sacred time, and cultural memory.
53. **Event vs. Trust** – Distinguishing spectacle from responsibility; sacred alignments are entrusted, not staged.

54. **Hierarchy (Dharmic)** – Natural ordering based on authenticity, discipline, and lived dharma.
55. **Memory (Smṛti)** – Active remembrance in ritual, landscape, and collective consciousness.
56. **Conscious Re-entry** – Mindful return of sacred time and practices into human life.
57. **Civilizational Flow / Living Tripod of Continuity** – Sustained cultural-spiritual current maintained by Youth, Scholars, and Institutions.
58. **River Warriors / Youth: Flame-Bearers** – Custodians of ritual, ecology, and memory.
59. **Transmission / Intergenerational Transmission** – Passing knowledge, practices, and sacred responsibility across generations.
60. **Ritual Integrity** – Faithful, conscious enactment of sacred practices aligned with ethics, ecology, and devotion.

Nilavilakku and Symbolism

61. **Nilavilakku** – Traditional Kerala oil lamp; embodies body, mind, intellect, and soul unified in fire.
62. **First Flame** – Inaugural lighting after centuries; reconnects present generation with ancestors.
63. **Bhu–Svarga Axis** – Vertical alignment between Earth and Heaven; established through ritual acts like Dhvaja-rohaṇa.
64. **Dhwajasthambam / Meru Daṇḍa** – Cosmic pillar reflected in temple flagstaff; axis of sacred space.
65. **Five Elements (Pañca Mahābhūtas)** – Earth, Water, Fire, Air, Space; converged in Nilavilakku ritual.

66. **Spanda** – Divine vibration; pulsation of sacred energy, civilization, and dharma.

Ethics, Lineage, and Remembrance

67. **Pitṛ / Pitṛ Loka** – Ancestors and their realm; active participants in sacred time.
68. **Pitṛ Ṛṇa / Deva Ṛṇa / Ṛṣi Ṛṇa** – Sacred debts to ancestors, divine forces, and sages.
69. **Avīra / Unremembered Dead** – Souls without descendants; ritual ensures their remembrance.
70. **Custodians of Memory** – Those performing Pitṛ Yajña and sustaining civilizational continuity.
71. **Remembrance as Healing** – Ritual memory transforms grief into wisdom and balance.

Key Mantras and Invocations

72. **Om Pūrṇamadaḥ Mantra** – Affirmation of infinite existence and continuity:
    "That is infinite. This is infinite. From the infinite, the infinite proceeds. Yet, the infinite remains."

BIBLIOGRAPHY

Primary Sanskrit Texts (Vedas, Upaniṣads, Purāṇas, and Smṛtis)

1. **Ṛg Veda**. Critical editions, Bhandarkar Oriental Research Institute / Vedic Research Institutes. Hymns relating to ṛta (cosmic order), Pitṛs, and temporal cycles.
2. **Yajur Veda** (Śukla & Kṛṣṇa recensions). Sections on Pitṛ Yajña, Tarpana, and śrāddha-related injunctions.
3. **Atharva Veda**. Hymns addressing ancestors, cosmic order, and collective ritual power.
4. **Śatapatha Brāhmaṇa**. Translated by Julius Eggeling. Oxford: Clarendon Press, 1882–1900. Ritual expositions on yajña, ṛta, and sacrifice.
5. **Taittirīya Saṁhitā & Taittirīya Brāhmaṇa**. Varanasi: Chowkhamba Sanskrit Series. Detailed discussions on ancestral rites and ritual orientation.
6. **Upaniṣads** (Bṛhadāraṇyaka, Chāndogya, Īśa, Kaṭha, Muṇḍaka). Translated with commentaries by Śaṅkarācārya. Various editions. Concepts of cosmic correspondence and temporal awareness.
7. **Bhagavad Gītā**. With Śaṅkara Bhāṣya. Emphasis on karma, yajña, dharma, and cyclical time.
8. **Mahābhārata**. Critical Edition. Pune: Bhandarkar Oriental Research Institute, 1927–1966. Śānti and Anuśāsana Parvas

on dharma, tīrthas, ancestral rites, and sacred temporality.

9. **Rāmāyaṇa**. Cultural geography and sacred river symbolism.
10. **Padma Purāṇa**. Critical editions and commentaries. Sections on Magha Māsa, snāna, and tīrtha-mahātmyas.
11. **Skanda Purāṇa**. Keralotpatti Khanda; Kāśī, Avanti, and Tīrtha-khaṇḍas. For sacred time, pilgrimage, and tīrtha theology.
12. **Bhāgavata Purāṇa**. Critical Edition with traditional commentaries. Cosmological symbolism, dharma, Samudra Manthana.
13. **Viṣṇu Purāṇa**. Translated by H. H. Wilson. London: Trübner & Co., 1840. Cosmology, avatars, and sacred geography.
14. **Kūrma Purāṇa**. Gita Press Edition. Mandara symbolism and Samudra Manthana.
15. **Matsya Purāṇa**. Trans. T. Ramachandra Dikshitar. Early cosmological narratives and temporal cycles.
16. **Bhaviṣya Purāṇa**. Calendrical sanctity and future sacred observances.
17. **Vāyu Purāṇa**. Cycles of time and ritual symbolism.
18. **Garuḍa Purāṇa**. Chapters on post-death states, Pitṛ-loka, and ancestral rites.
19. **Manusmṛti & Yājñavalkya Smṛti**. Ritual discipline, ancestral duty, and civilizational continuity.
20. **Nārada Smṛti**. Vrata, dāna, snāna, and Pitṛ obligations.
21. **Āpastamba Dharma Sūtra & Baudhāyana Dharma Sūtra**. Household rituals and ancestral rites.

Jyotiṣa, Calendrical, and Astronomical Texts

22. Varāhamihira. **Bṛhat Saṁhitā**. Translated by H. Kern. Planetary cycles, auspicious alignments, and sacred temporality.

23. Parāśara. **Bṛhat Parāśara Horā Śāstra**. Jupiter cycles, cosmic timing, and dharmic alignment.

24. E. Burgess. **Sūrya Siddhānta**. Classical astronomical framework for solar-lunar cycles.

25. **Vedāṅga Jyotiṣa**. Critical editions. Foundations of Vedic calendrical science.

26. Pañcāṅga Traditions (North & South India). Lunar-solar calculations governing Magha, Nakṣatra alignments, and Kumbha timing.

27. Mantreśvara. **Phaladīpikā**. Planetary influence on collective ritual and psychology.

Commentarial and Philosophical Literature

28. Śaṅkarācārya. *Bhāṣyas & Vivekacūḍāmaṇi*. Liberation as alignment, recognition, and ethical continuity.

29. Medhātithi. Commentary on Manusmṛti. Interpretive clarity on ritual time and ethics.

30. Vijñāneśvara. *Mitākṣarā*. Smṛti interpretation and social-spiritual integration.

31. Mīmāṁsā Sūtras of Jaimini. Ritual efficacy, unseen results (apūrva), and dharmic continuity.

32. Eliade, Mircea. *The Sacred and the Profane: The Nature of Religion*. New York: Harcourt, 1959. Sacred time and hierophany.

33. Eliade, Mircea. *Myth and Reality*. New York: Harper & Row, 1963. Myth as reactivated sacred history.

34. Eliade, Mircea. *Myth of the Eternal Return.* Princeton University Press, 1954. Cyclical renewal and sacred temporality.

35. Zimmer, Heinrich. *Myths and Symbols in Indian Art and Civilization.* Princeton University Press, 1946. Symbolic cosmology and ritual intelligence.

36. Zimmer, Heinrich. *Philosophies of India.* Princeton University Press, 1951. Cyclical time and civilizational memory.

37. Coomaraswamy, Ananda K. *Hinduism and Buddhism.* New York: Philosophical Library. Symbols, cosmology, and dharmic order.

38. Coomaraswamy, Ananda K. *Time and Eternity.* Princeton University Press. Metaphysics of cyclical continuity.

39. Feuerstein, Georg. *The Yoga Tradition.* Sacred time, tapas, and altered consciousness.

40. Kramrisch, Stella. *The Presence of Śiva.* Princeton University Press, 1981.

41. Kramrisch, Stella. *The Hindu Temple,* Vols. I–II. Motilal Banarsidass. Temple cosmology and sacred alignment.

42. P. V. Kane. *History of Dharmaśāstra,* Vols. I–V. Bhandarkar Oriental Research Institute. Ritual and dharmic order.

Studies on Pilgrimage, Rivers, and Sacred Geography

43. Diana L. Eck. *India: A Sacred Geography.* New York: Harmony Books, 2012. Rivers, tīrthas, and lived sacred landscapes.

44. Bharati, Agehananda. *The Tantric Tradition.* New York: Samuel Weiser, 1975. Ritual symbolism and sacred temporality.

45. Lochtefeld, James G. *God's Gateway: Identity and Meaning in a Hindu Pilgrimage Place*. Oxford University Press, 2010.

46. Kumar, Ravindra. *Kumbh Mela: Mapping the Ephemeral Megacity*. Harvard University Press, 2015.

47. Kinsley, David. *Hindu Gods and Goddesses: Visions of the Divine*. Berkeley: University of California Press, 1988.

48. Gadgil, Madhav & Ramachandra Guha. *Ecology and Equity: The Use and Abuse of Nature in Contemporary India*. Penguin India.

49. Gadgil, Madhav & Ramachandra Guha. *This Fissured Land: An Ecological History of India*. Oxford University Press.

50. Chapple, Christopher Key. *Hinduism and Ecology*. Harvard University Press, 2000.

51. Haberman, David. *River of Love in an Age of Pollution: The Yamuna River of Northern India*. University of California Press, 2006.

52. David Frawley (Vāmadeva Śāstrī). *Hinduism and Ecology*.

Kerala, Bharathapuzha, and Regional History

53. Ayyappan, A. *Social Revolution in Kerala*. Asia Publishing House, 1968.

54. Menon, A. Sreedhara. *A Survey of Kerala History*. DC Books.

55. Panikkar, K. M. *A History of Kerala*. Annamalai University, 1960.

56. K. P. Padmanabha Menon. *History of Kerala*, Vols. 1–2. Madras: Cochin Government Press, 1924.

57. M. G. S. Narayanan. *Perumals of Kerala*. Calicut University, 1996.

58. M. G. S. Narayanan. *Cultural Symbiosis in Kerala.*

59. Kerala State Gazetteers: Palakkad, Thrissur, Malappuram Districts. Government of Kerala.

60. M. T. Vasudevan Nair. Selected essays and reflections on Bharathapuzha.

Ascetic, Āśrama, and Living Traditions

61. Swami Sivananda. *Sādhanā and Practice of Brahmacharya.*

62. Agehananda Bharati. *The Ochre Robe.*

63. Gavin Flood. *The Ascetic Self.*

64. Mircea Eliade. *Yoga: Immortality and Freedom.*

65. Patrick Olivelle. *The Āśrama System: The History and Hermeneutics of a Religious Institution.* Oxford University Press.

66. Oral traditions of riverine communities along Bharathapuzha.

Ritual, Magha, and Maha Magha Studies

67. Temple ritual manuals (Āgamas, Kṣetra-Paddhatis) – Kerala and Kashi traditions.

68. Oral instructions of traditional Paṇḍits and Tīrtha-Purohits regarding Magha Snāna, Pitṛ-kārya, and Vrata observances.

69. Tantrāloka – Abhinavagupta. Spanda, ritual consciousness, and awakening śakti.

70. Ṣaṭcakra Nirūpaṇa, Śiva Saṁhitā, Haṭha Yoga Pradīpikā. River symbolism, internal pilgrimage, and sacred flow.

Civilizational Perspectives and Contemporary Reflections

71. Rajiv Malhotra. *Being Different: An Indian Challenge to Western Universalism*. HarperCollins India, 2011.
72. Dharampal. *Indian Science and Technology in the Eighteenth Century*.
73. Satish Kumar. *Soil, Soul, Society*.
74. E. F. Schumacher. *Small Is Beautiful*.
75. Vandana Shiva. Selected writings on rivers and sacred ecology.
76. Romila Thapar. Selected works on sacred geography, time, and historical memory.
77. Charles Malamoud. *Cooking the World: Ritual and Thought in Ancient India*.

ANNEXURE: KERALA'S KUMBH MELA

Maha Magha—Kerala's Sacred Kumbh Mela

1. Overview

Maha Magha is a sacred convergence of faith, memory, and civilizational continuity, celebrated on the banks of the *Bharathapuzha*—the Dakṣiṇa Gaṅgā. It is the *South's sacred Kumbh,* a spiritual axis where rivers, rituals, and devotion align to restore the ancient rhythm of Dharma. The Maha Magha Mela is not merely a festival; it is a living tradition, a time when the sacred and the secular merge, and the pilgrim becomes the participant in the cosmic dance of time.

2. Period of the Mela

Maha Magha is observed during the Magha month of the Hindu calendar, when the Magha Nakshatra aligns with the full moon, and the sacred waters of Bharathapuzha are believed to possess profound purifying power. The Mela spans the entire Magha month, with the peak days occurring on:

1. Magha Purnima (Full Moon Day)
2. Magha Amavasya (New Moon Day)
3. Magha Nakshatra days (especially the day of Magha Nakshatra)

The Mela period is a time of collective sadhana, when the river becomes a living witness to devotion, penance, and remembrance.

3. Inauguration of the Mela

The Maha Magha Mela begins with a sacred opening ceremony that aligns the community with the purpose of the festival: recollection, renewal, and reverence.

Key elements of the inauguration:

1. *Pūjā and Invocation:* The Mela is inaugurated with traditional pūjā performed by the priests, invoking the blessings of Lord Śiva, Devi Śakti, and the River Goddess.

2. *Lighting of the First Flame (Nilavilakku):* The lighting of the First Flame symbolizes the return of the sacred rhythm after centuries of silence. It is a sacred affirmation that the ancient tradition is alive again.

3. *Hoisting of the Dharma Dhvaja:* The Dharma Dhvaja (flag of Dharma) is raised as a civilizational declaration—an emblem of continuity, unity, and spiritual resolve.

4. *Sankalpa and Blessings:* Saints, sages, scholars, and devotees participate in the collective sankalpa (vow) to preserve the sanctity of the Mela and live its principles beyond the festival.

4. Daily Schedule and Rituals

The Maha Magha Mela is a living tapestry of ritual, devotion, and sacred learning. Each day follows a rhythm that aligns the pilgrim with the cosmic flow of time.

Daily Rituals:

4.1. Brahma Muhurta Sadhana:

1. **Time:** Early morning (before sunrise)
2. **Practices:** Meditation, chanting of Vedic mantras, and silent contemplation beside the river.
3. **Purpose:** To attune the mind to the purity of dawn and to open the heart to divine grace.

4.2. Nila Arati (The River's Lamp):

1. **Time:** Evening
2. **Practice:** Lighting of lamps on the riverbank, accompanied by sacred chants and hymns.
3. **Significance:** The river is honored as the living Dakṣiṇa Gaṅgā; the light symbolizes remembrance and continuity.

4.3. Magha Snāna (Sacred Bath):

1. **Time:** Peak hours during the day
2. **Practice:** Pilgrims immerse themselves in the river, offering prayers and mantras.
3. **Meaning:** The bath is not merely physical purification but spiritual renewal—an alignment of body, mind, and soul.

4.4. Pitr Yajña (Ancestor Worship):

1. **Practice:** Offering tarpan, recitation of mantras, and rituals to honor ancestors.
2. The ritual heals historical rupture and restores familial and civilizational memory.

4.5. Bhakti Sadhana and Kirtan:

1. **Practice:** Singing devotional hymns, bhajans, and kirtans, often continuing late into the night.
2. **Significance:** The devotional energy becomes a collective current of grace.

5. Major Programs and Events

The Mela is not only a ritual space but also a hub of spiritual learning and civilizational revival. Major programs include:

5.1. Vedic Discourses and Spiritual Lectures:

Renowned scholars and saints deliver discourses on:

1. Maha Magha's mythic and historical significance
2. Advaita Vedanta and the philosophy of grace
3. The sacred geography of Bharathapuzha
4. The Agastya Principle and the Dakṣiṇa Kumbh are key concepts in this section.

5.2. Tantric and Śakti Traditions:

Workshops and discussions highlight:

1. The living tradition of Tantra in the South
2. The worship of Śakti and the feminine divine

3. Rituals of preservation and continuity

5.3. Cultural Performances:

Classical music, dance, and devotional art forms are presented as offerings to the river and the divine.

5.4. Yoga, Meditation, and Spiritual Retreats:

Guided sessions for inner alignment, including:

1. Yoga practices
2. Breathwork and mindfulness
3. Silent retreats

5.5. Community and Service:

The Mela also includes:

1. Community feeding (Annadanam)
2. Cleanliness drives along the riverbanks
3. Spiritual outreach and support for pilgrims

6. Winding Up the Mela

The conclusion of Maha Magha is not an end but a transition—a return to ordinary life while carrying the sacred rhythm within.

Closing Rituals:

1. *Final Nila Arati and Homam*: The river is honored once again through lamps and fire offerings, marking the end of the festival cycle.

2. *Dharma Dhvaja Lowering Ceremony:* The flag is respectfully lowered, signifying the closing of the sacred gathering while preserving the spirit of the vow.

3. *Collective Sankalpa for Continuity*: Pilgrims take a vow to carry the principles of Maha Magha into daily life: ecological responsibility, ethical living, and spiritual remembrance.

4. *Departure with Blessings:* Devotees leave with renewed purpose, carrying the memory of the river's grace into their homes and communities.

7. Significance of the Schedule

The schedule of Maha Magha is designed not merely as a series of events, but as a rhythm of alignment—a sacred cycle that synchronizes the individual with the river, the land, and the cosmic time. Each ritual is a step toward the restoration of civilizational memory and the rekindling of the Dakṣiṇa's spiritual gravity.

<u>OFFICIAL BROACHER:</u>

Kerala's "Kumbh Mela"

(will be celebrated with great splendor from January 18 to February 3 in Thirunavaya)

This festival, popularly known as "Mamankam," is considered Kerala's version of the Kumbh Mela.

According to legend, the first sacrificial rite (yajna) for the welfare of the world was performed by Parashurama on the banks of the Bharathapuzha at Thirunavaya, in a place called Tapasunur, now known as Thavunur. All the gods are said to have attended this yajna, which was conducted under Brahma's direction as per Parashurama's instructions. The sacrificial month of Magha, when the seven sacred rivers converge in the Bharathapuzha (known as Dakshina Ganga), is considered especially auspicious.

The yajna is believed to be repeated every twelve years, giving rise to the Mahamagh Mahotsavam. After the first yajna performed by Brahma, the deity Brihaspati (the guru of the gods) became the first chairman of the festival. Over time, when divine kings ruled the land, the position of chairman was handed over to the Perumals (local rulers), and Brihaspati withdrew. Every twelve years, this cultural festival was held on the banks of the Nila River, showcasing all forms of Kerala's art, various martial demonstrations, scholarly discourses, and scientific discussions. It also evolved into a major commercial fair of South India.

All the kings of Kerala would gather at the Thirunavaya Mahamagh Mahotsavam, presenting the accounts of their twelve-year reign before their patron deity. The festival also served as a platform for astrologers to predict upcoming climatic changes and advise on agriculture and lifestyle, and to appoint the next Perumal (ruler) for the next twelve years.

However, after the last Perumal, Cheraman Perumal, left the world from the Thiruvanchikulam Shiva temple with Sundaramurti Nayanar, the festival lost its royal patron. The Kochi-based Perumbadappu Swaroopam then took over the chairmanship and appointed Valluvanadu's king, Valluvakkonathiri, as its representative. Later, Samutiri (the Zamorin) seized the chairmanship from Valluvakkonathiri, leading to a period of rivalry between the two royal houses. The "Mamankam" that followed, marked by bloodshed, ended about 250years ago.

In recent years, inspired by divine intervention, efforts have been made to revive this cultural festival. During the last Prayagraj Kumbh Mela, Swami Anandavan Bharati Maharaj, a senior monk of the Junagadh Akhada, was appointed as the Mahamandaleshwar (chief) for South India. Recognizing the need to revive the ancient Mahamagh Mahotsavam held at Thirunavaya, he decided to organize the event on a grand scale, calling it "Kerala's Kumbh Mela."

The current Mahamagh Mahotsavam is presented as a call to defend Sanatan (eternal) culture against growing challenges. It begins with prayers for the souls of the countless warriors who died in the Mamankam battles, seeking their liberation. Sacred lamps from the four Ambika temples established by Parashurama for the protection of Kerala will be brought to the festival venue.

The Bharathapuzha, known as Dakshina Ganga, originates from Thirumurti Hills near Udumalpet in TamilNadu. The hills are associated with the sage Atri and his wife, Anasuya; the Trimurti (Brahma, Vishnu, and Shiva) are said to have appeared there, giving the place its name. It is also the birthplace of Dattatreya, the deity of the Junagadh Akhada.

A chariot procession (rathayatra) will start from Thirumurti

Hills on January 19, travel through Udumalpet, Pellachi, Etta Madu, Coimbatore, and other places, and enter Kerala at Palakkad, Thrissur, Shoranur, and Ottapalam before reaching Thirunavaya on January 22. On the same day, the "Dharmadhvaja Arohanam" (hoisting of the sacred flag) will take place at Thirunavaya.

Every day of the festival, the beautiful "Nila Arathi" (worship of the Nila River) will be performed on the banks of the Bharathapuzha. This year, members of all royal families of Kerala, as well as monks from every Kerala math (monastic institution) and from Tamil Nadu, Karnataka, Andhra Pradesh, and Maharashtra, will participate. Followers of all Hindu traditions will conduct their respective rituals and offer prayers.

Special days observed during the festival include Mouni Amavasya, Vasant Panchami, Rathasapthami, Ganesh Jayanti, Shashthi, Bhishmashtami, and Magha Purnima. Bathing in the Bharathapuzha during the Magha month, especially on these sacred days, is considered highly meritorious, as is bathing together with saintly persons.

The Mahamagh Mahotsavam at Thirunavaya, hailed as Kerala's Kumbh Mela, invites everyone to partake in its spiritual and cultural grandeur.

- Convenor, Mahamagh Mahotsavam Committee

Brochure Summary & Key Details

Below is a summary of the official schedule and details as presented in the festival literature for immediate reference.

Event Title: Thirunavaya Mahamagha Mahotsavam 2026 (Kerala Kumbh Mela)

Period: January 18, 2026 – February 3, 2026

Location: Sacred Banks of the Bharathapuzha (Nila River), Thirunavaya Navamukunda Temple Grounds, Malappuram District, Kerala.

Core Schedule & Rituals:

1. **Magha Snanam (Holy Bath):** Daily from 6:00 AM to 6:00 PM.

2. **Nila Aarti:** Daily evening worship of the river (modeled on the Ganga Aarti of Kashi), performed by priests from Varanasi and Kerala.

3. **Yajna & Homam:** Daily Vedic sacrifices for global peace and pitru (ancestral) liberation.

A. INAUGURATION DAY SCHEDULE

Date: 19 January 2026 (Monday)

Time	Programme	Location
5:00 AM	Brahma Muhūrta Snāna & Silent Japa	River Ghats
6:30 AM	Vedic Pūjā to Bharathapuzha	Main Ghat
8:00 AM	Collective Sankalpa by Saints & Organisers	Yajña Śālā
9:30 AM	**Lighting of the First Flame (Nilavilakku)**	Sacred Stage

10:00 AM	**Dharma Dhvaja-rohaṇa (Hoisting of the Flag)**	Flag Mast Area
10:30 AM	Inaugural Blessings & Discourses	Main Pavilion
1:00 PM	Annadānam	Community Dining Area
6:30 PM	**Nila Ārati (River Lamp Offering)**	Riverbank
7:30 PM	Bhakti Kīrtana & Cultural Offerings	Open Stage

B. DAILY RITUAL SCHEDULE (20 Jan – 1 Feb 2026)

Time	Daily Ritual	Description
4:30 AM	Brahma Muhūrta Sādhana	Meditation, Mantra Japa
5:30 AM	Magha Snāna	Sacred Bath in Bharathapuzha
7:00 AM	Vedic Chanting & Pūjā	River & Yajña Śālā
9:00 AM	Spiritual Discourses	Scholars, Sages
12:30 PM	Annadānam	Seva to Pilgrims
3:00 PM	Tantra–Śakti Sessions	South Indian Traditions

5:30 PM	Yoga & Dhyāna	Open Grounds
6:30 PM	Nila Ārati	Riverbank
7:30 PM	Bhajans, Kīrtans, Cultural Programmes	Main Stage

C. SPECIAL SACRED DAYS

Date	**Significance**	**Special Observances**
23 Jan 2026	Magha Nakṣatra Day	Mass Snāna & Pitr Tarpana
29 Jan 2026	Amāvāsyā	Ancestor Rituals (Pitṛ Yajña)
2 Feb 2026	**Magha Pūrṇimā**	Maha Snāna & Closing Sankalpa

D. MAGHA PŪRṆIMĀ – GRAND CONCLUSION

Date: 2 February 2026 (Monday)

Time	**Programme**	**Location**
4:30 AM	Maha Magha Snāna	Main River Ghat
7:00	Final Pūjā & Homam	Yajña Śālā

AM		
10:00 AM	Collective Gratitude Prayers	Main Pavilion
12:00 PM	Mahā Annadānam	Community Grounds
5:30 PM	Final Nila Ārati	Bharathapuzha
6:30 PM	Lowering of Dharma Dhvaja	Flag Area
7:00 PM	Closing Sankalpa & Blessings	Sacred Stage

E. CONTINUITY DECLARATION

The Maha Magha Mahotsavam formally concludes, yet the sacred rhythm continues—
as remembrance, ecological reverence, ancestral harmony, and lived Dharma.

Note: This schedule reflects the **civilizational rhythm** of Maha Magha. Minor variations may occur in alignment with lunar calculations and local traditions.

DAYS OF SACRED IMPORTANCE

Maha Magha Mahotsavam | January 18 – February 3, 2026

January 18—Mauni Amavasya

The Silence of Origins and Ancestors

Mauni Amavasya, the sacred new moon preceding Mahāśivarātri, is a day devoted to silence, remembrance, and ancestral grace. Tradition holds that on this day Swayambhuva Manu, the first progenitor of humanity, descended upon the earth, marking the beginning of the human lineage. Hence, Mauni Amavasya is both a cosmic birthday of mankind and a day of Pitṛ Smaraṇa.

It is believed that on this day the ancestors (*pitṛs*) are especially receptive. Performing Pitṛ Pūjā, remembering forefathers with gratitude, and observing *mauna* (silence) dissolves inherited karmic burdens. Silence on this day is not emptiness but receptivity—answers to life's unresolved questions are said to arise from this profound stillness.

A sacred bath in the holy river Bharathapuzha on Mauni Amavasya, accompanied by ancestral remembrance, is believed to cleanse generational afflictions and invite prosperity, harmony, and peace. The Maha Magha Mahotsavam at Thirunavaya formally begins on this sacred day, grounding the festival in remembrance before celebration.

January 19—Beginning of Magha Gupta Navaratri

The Nine Nights of Hidden Power

Magha Gupta Navaratri marks the commencement of a deeply inward and esoteric observance dedicated to the Ten Mahāvidyās of Goddess Durga. Known also as Śiśira Navaratri, it is called "Gupta" (hidden) because its worship is not outwardly displayed but performed in silence, secrecy, and disciplined restraint. This Navaratri is considered the most potent period for tantric sādhana, mantra japa, meditation, and inner purification. Spiritual practices begun on this day are believed to calm disturbances of vāta, pitta, and kapha, restoring both physical balance and mental clarity.

Among all Navaratris—Vasanta, Ashada, Sharada, and Magha—the Magha Gupta Navaratri is regarded as the most powerful for secret spiritual disciplines. Since these days coincide with subtle movements of divine feminine energies in nature, devotees are advised to undertake fasting and holy river baths to attune themselves to these forces.

January 19—Dharma Dhvaja Rōhaṇam

The Flag of Revival and Continuity

On this historic day, the Dharma Dhvaja (Sacred Flag) of Maha Magha is ceremonially hoisted at Thirunavaya, proclaiming the return of a tradition that had remained dormant for over two and a half centuries.

The raising of the flag is not a mere ritual announcement—it is a declaration that river worship, Nīlā Ārati, sacred bathing, yajñas, and dharmic observances have re-entered living time. The Dharma Dhvaja signifies the redemption of forgotten history, the return of divine rhythms, and the restoration of a dharma-centered way of life.

With this act, the land itself is reminded of its sacred responsibility.

January 19—Rathayātra from Thirumurtimala

Reuniting Source and Sacred Destination

The Rathayātra of Maha Magha begins at Thirumurtimala near Udumalpet in Tamil Nadu, close to the source of the Bharathapuzha. After Śrī Cakra Pūjā at the Amanalingeśvara Temple on the riverbank, the chariot bearing the Mahāmeru begins its sacred journey.

Passing through Udumalpet, Pollachi, Coimbatore, Ettimadai,

Palakkad, Kalpathy, Shoranur, and Ottapalam, the Rathayātra reaches Thirunavaya on January 22. This journey symbolically reunites the river's origin with its sacred confluence, healing the fractured sacred geography of the land.

January 19—Navakoti Ashtākṣara Mantra Japam

A Collective Yajña of Divine Sound

At the spiritual heart of Maha Magha Mahotsavam lies the Navakoti Ashtākṣara Mantra Japam—a collective vow to complete nine crore (90 million) repetitions of the sacred mantra:

"Om Namo Nārāyaṇāya"

This mantra, revered as the Tāraka Mantra in the Vaishnava tradition, is believed to grant liberation and divine protection. At Thirunavaya, the abode of Lord Navamukunda, its potency is considered unparalleled.

The number nine (*nava*) symbolizes completeness—reflecting the Navagrahas, Navavidha Bhakti, and the nine gateways of the human body. The Japam is performed through:

1. **Vācika Japam** (group chanting at riverbanks and temples)
2. **Likhita Japam** (writing the mantra as a meditative discipline)

The collective vibration is believed to cleanse the ether (*ākāśa śuddhi*), stabilize the spiritual energy of the land, and restore the forgotten sanctity of Dakṣiṇa Kāśī. Even a single chant, offered sincerely, is said to partake in the merit of the whole.

January 19–20—Ganapati Homam & Bhagavathi Seva

Opening the Path, Guarding the Night

These two rituals form the spiritual axis of daily worship at Maha Magha.

1. Ganapati Homam (Morning): Performed during Brahma Muhūrta, this fire ritual invokes Lord Gaṇeśa, the remover of obstacles. Thousands of coconuts—symbols of the ego—are offered into the sacred fire. The rising smoke purifies the atmosphere and clears both visible and subtle impediments, ensuring the smooth unfolding of the Mahotsavam.

2. Bhagavathi Seva (Evening): Conducted after sunset, this Kerala Tantric ritual invokes the Divine Mother through lamp worship. A sacred Padmam (lotus diagram) is drawn, and the Goddess is invoked into a central lamp. This ritual offers protection, peace, and maternal grace, spiritually safeguarding pilgrims resting along the riverbanks.

Together, these rituals complete a sacred circle—Gaṇeśa opens the way at dawn, and the Mother stands guard at dusk.

January 20 & 21—Navakoti Ashtākṣara Mantra Japam

The Sound That Rebuilds the Sacred Field

These two days are devoted to the continuation and intensification of the Navakoti Ashtākṣara Mantra Japam, the spiritual backbone of the Maha Magha Mahotsavam. This observance is not an isolated ritual but a Maha Yajña of collective consciousness, undertaken for Loka Kalyāṇa—the welfare and harmony of the world.

The Mantra and Its Power

At the heart of this Japam resounds the eight-syllabled sacred formula:

"Om Namo Nārāyaṇāya"

—revered as the *Tāraka Mantra*, the liberating sound that carries the soul across cycles of birth and death. At Thirunavaya, the sacred seat of Lord Navamukunda, this mantra is believed to awaken its fullest protective and sustaining force.

Why 'Navakoti'—Nine Crores

The number nine (*nava*) signifies wholeness and completion in Vedic thought—echoing the Navagrahas, Navavidha Bhakti, and the nine openings of the human body. Completing nine crore chants collectively allows thousands of individual voices to dissolve into a single current of divine vibration, restoring harmony to land, water, and ether.

Practice and Participation

The Japam unfolds through:

1. **Vācika Japam**—collective chanting at dawn along the riverbanks and temple precincts
2. **Likhita Japam**—writing the mantra, aligning mind, speech, and body (*tri-karaṇa śuddhi*)

Spiritual Impact

It is believed that the cumulative resonance purifies the subtle atmosphere (*ākāśa śuddhi*), dissolving historical stagnation and re-establishing Thirunavaya as Dakṣiṇa Kāśī. Even a single chant, offered sincerely, shares the merit of the whole—like a drop becoming the ocean.

January 22—Gaṇeśa Jayantī

The Birth of Auspicious Beginnings

Gaṇeśa Jayantī, observed on the Śukla Pakṣa Caturthī of

Magha, commemorates the cosmic birth of Lord Gaṇeśa, the presiding intelligence of beginnings, thresholds, and obstacles. Also known as Tilakunda Caturthī, this day marks Gaṇeśa's emergence in the outer universe, while Gaṇeśa Caturthī (later in the year) marks his descent upon the earth.

Gaṇeśa is the power that both creates and dissolves obstacles, reminding devotees that this intelligence resides within the self. On Gaṇeśa Jayantī, nature itself undergoes subtle energetic shifts—especially within water bodies, which absorb and transmit these changes.

Importance of the Holy Bath

The human body (*piṇḍāṇḍa*) mirrors the cosmos (*brahmāṇḍa*). Bathing in the river that has absorbed these cosmic vibrations awakens Gaṇeśa within the seeker, aligning inner and outer nature. A sacred dip on this day is believed to invite prosperity, clarity, and auspicious movement in life.

The Gaṇeśa Jayantī Snāna at Bharathapuzha will be observed on this day at the Maha Magha Mahotsavam.

January 23—Vasant Pañcamī

When Knowledge Blossoms Like Spring

Vasant Pañcamī, also known as Śrī Pañcamī or Sarasvatī Pañcamī, falls on the fifth day of the waxing moon in Magha. It heralds the arrival of spring, when seeds hidden beneath the soil begin to stir toward life.

This day is infused with Sarasvatī tattva—the subtle intelligence governing learning, creativity, speech, and insight. The Moon, associated with imagination and reflection, is especially potent on this Pañcamī; thoughts formed today are believed to grow and flower with ease.

Spiritual and Cultural Significance

Across much of India, children are initiated into learning on this day. For poets, artists, scholars, and seekers of wisdom, a holy bath on Vasant Pañcamī is considered especially auspicious. On this day, the Bharathapuzha is believed to flow with the living presence of Sarasvatī, making the river bath a sacrament of awakening knowledge.

Vasant Pañcamī Snāna at Thirunavaya will be observed on January 23.

January 24—Makhaṣaṣṭhī (Magha Śukla Ṣaṣṭh ī)

The Day of the Divine Warrior

Makhaṣaṣṭhī is dedicated to Lord Subrahmaṇya (Murugan / Kārtikeya), the divine commander of celestial forces and the embodiment of disciplined courage. In the spiritual traditions of South India, this day is a call to inner valor.

The Spear of Wisdom (Vel)

The central symbol of the day is the Vel, not merely a weapon but the piercing force of jñāna śakti. On Makhaṣaṣṭhī, the Vel is believed to cut through ignorance (*avidyā*), just as Murugan vanquished the demon Tārakāsura.

Rituals and Observances

1. **Upavāsa and Mauna** to cultivate inner discipline
2. **Abhiṣekam and Kavadi offerings** at temporary shrines
3. **Nāga Ārādhana**, reflecting Murugan's deep connection to serpent symbolism and ancestral healing

Spiritual Essence

Makhaṣaṣṭhī reminds the pilgrim that spiritual life demands alertness and strength. Dharma must be guarded. The lamps lit for Murugan on the banks of the Nila burn with sharp clarity—focused, fearless, and resolute.

January 25—Ratha Saptamī

The Birth of the Inner Sun

Ratha Saptamī, the seventh day of the bright fortnight of Magha, celebrates the manifestation of the Sun (Sūrya) in a darkened universe. Born to Sage Kaśyapa and Aditi, the Sun is revered as Sūrya-Nārāyaṇa, the luminous aspect of Viṣṇu.

On this day, the Sun turns northward (*Uttarāyaṇa*), marking the gradual awakening of warmth, vitality, and growth—both in nature and consciousness.

Symbolism of the Solar Chariot

1. **Seven horses** represent the days of the week and seven rays of light.
2. **Twelve wheels** signify the zodiac and the cycles of time.

Spiritual Importance

Worship of the sun on this day is believed to ignite the inner sun, dispelling darkness of ignorance, disease, and despair. Chanting Āditya Hṛdayam, Sūrya Aṣṭakam, and Sūrya Kavacam, followed by a sacred river bath, is considered transformative—especially for health, confidence, leadership, and vitality.

The Ratha Saptamī Snāna at Bharathapuzha will be observed on January 25.

January 26—Bhīṣmāṣṭamī

The Departure of Dharma Itself

Bhīṣmāṣṭamī commemorates the sacred departure of Bhīṣma Pitāmaha, the embodiment of unwavering dharma. Endowed with *icchā-mṛtyu* (the boon of choosing the moment of death), Bhīṣma waited upon his bed of arrows for the sun's northward journey—*Uttarāyaṇa*, when the devas are awake.

On the Aṣṭamī of Magha, he relinquished his body after imparting the Viṣṇu Sahasranāma to Yudhiṣṭhira, sealing the Mahābhārata with the essence of devotion and surrender.

Spiritual Significance

Uttarāyaṇa is considered a divine dawn. Japa, meditation, fasting, and sacred bathing performed during this period are said to yield multiplied spiritual merit. A holy dip on Bhīṣmāṣṭamī, accompanied by Viṣṇu Sahasranāma chanting, is believed to bestow liberation and Vaishnava grace.

The Bhīṣmāṣṭamī Snāna at Bharathapuzha will be observed on January 26, marking a day when dharma itself blesses the river and those who enter it.

January 27 – Mahananda Navami

The Ninth Wave of Auspicious Fulfillment

Mahananda Navami falls on the ninth day of the Shukla Paksha in the holy month of Magha and marks the culmination of the *Magha Gupta Navaratri*—the Nine Nights of Hidden Worship. This day is dedicated equally to Goddess Durga, the power that removes obstacles and enemies, and Goddess Lakshmi, the source of abundance and stability.

Scriptural tradition affirms that when the Magha Gupta Navaratri is observed with discipline until Mahananda Navami, the spiritual merit equals that of performing an Ashwamedha Yagna, the highest royal sacrifice of ancient times.

On this day, the energies of victory, prosperity, and inner assurance reach a peak. Bathing in sacred rivers is believed to dissolve poverty, subdue adversarial forces—both external and internal—and remove stagnation in life.

At Thirunavaya, the Mahananda Snanam in the Bharathapuzha becomes a prayer in motion, aligning the devotee with divine assurance and fulfillment.

January 28 – Gupta Vijayadashami

The Silent Triumph of Inner Victory

Gupta Vijayadashami marks the completion of the *Magha Gupta Navaratri*. Unlike the public celebrations of Vijayadashami in the autumn, this observance is inward, secretive, and deeply transformative.

The term *Gupta* signifies "hidden." During these nine nights, ascetics and seekers worship the ten Mahavidyas, the esoteric wisdom forms of the Divine Mother. Their practices are unseen, intense, and aimed not at display, but at self-conquest.

On Gupta Vijayadashami:

1. Secret fire rituals receive their *Purnahuti* (final offering).
2. Ascetics emerge from silence, having subdued the mind and senses.
3. The atmosphere itself is believed to be charged with siddhic energy.

For pilgrims, this is a rare day of grace—when the accumulated tapas of saints flows outward to the world. It teaches that the greatest victories are those won within, beyond applause and recognition.

January 29 – Jaya Ekadashi

The Ekadashi That Grants Both Liberation and Merit

Jaya Ekadashi is celebrated as the Ekadashi that not only destroys sins but also bestows virtue. Its significance is revealed in the *Bhavishya Purana* through a dialogue between Lord Krishna and Yudhishthira.

The legend speaks of two cursed Gandharvas who unknowingly observed this Ekadashi through fasting, reflection, and restraint. Without awareness, they attained merit, were freed from their curse, and returned to divine realms.

Thus, Jaya Ekadashi holds a unique promise:

1. Even unintentional observance bears fruit.
2. Ghostly afflictions and unseen fears are dissolved.
3. Liberation (Vaikuntha Prapti) is attainable.

At Maha Magha Mahotsavam, bathing in the Bharathapuzha on this day allows every pilgrim—householder or ascetic—to partake in this current of redemption.

January 30 – Magha Dwadashi

The Day of Completion, Charity, and Nourishment

Magha Dwadashi follows the austerity of Ekadashi and signifies divine acceptance of the devotee's penance. Dedicated to Lord

Madhava (Vishnu), it is the day when fasting is ceremonially broken (*Parana*) and blessings are sealed.

Sesame (*Til*) plays a central role:

1. Used in ritual bathing,
2. Offered in sacred fire,
3. Donated as charity.

Sesame symbolizes karmic release and ancestral upliftment.

The hallmark of this day is Annadanam—feeding pilgrims and sadhus. The banks of the Nila transform into a sacred dining hall where distinctions vanish. Feeding another is equated with worshipping Narayana Himself.

The lesson of Magha Dwadashi is clear:
Spiritual discipline matures into compassionate service.

January 31 – Magha Trayodashi (Pradosha Vrata)

Twilight Worship of Lord Shiva

Magha Trayodashi is sacred to Lord Shiva, observed during *Pradosha Kala*—the twilight period when cosmic energies are in balance. Tradition holds that Shiva dances the *Ananda Tandava* at this time to calm the universe.

Rituals include:

1. Abhishekam of the Shiva Linga,
2. Silent meditation,
3. Special worship of Nandi, the symbol of the disciplined mind.

Prayers whispered into Nandi's ears are believed to reach Shiva directly.

This day purifies the devotee before the fullness of Magha Purnima, emptying the heart of karmic residue so it may receive grace completely.

February 01 – Magha Purnima & Thaipooyam

The Zenith of Light and Devotion

Magha Purnima is the spiritual summit of the Maha Magha Mahotsavam. The full moon in the Magha constellation floods the Bharathapuzha with lunar energy, while Thaipooyam ignites the land with Murugan's fiery devotion.

1. Maha Shahi Snan is performed at moonrise.
2. Pilgrims enter the river in unison—saints, seekers, and householders alike.
3. Kavadi processions fill the banks with rhythm, trance, and surrender.

This day unites:

1. Vishnu's cooling grace,
2. Shiva's ascetic depth,
3. Murugan's protective fire.

Standing in the river under the full moon, the pilgrim experiences the dissolution of duality—only light remains.

February 02 – Magha Chaturdashi & Desha Deva Puja

Invocation of the Cosmic Trinity and Guardian Deities

Magha Chaturdashi honors:

1. ***Brahma*** – Creator,
2. ***Vishnu*** – Preserver,
3. ***Maheswara (Shiva)*** – Dissolver.

Alongside the Trimurti, the Desha Devas—guardian deities of the land—are worshipped, acknowledging that sacred geography itself sustains the Mela.

Special reverence is offered to:

1. **Thrippangottappan** – Shiva as the conqueror of death,
2. **Thali Thevar**—the silent witness of Mamankam history.

This day dissolves sectarian boundaries, affirming that all paths lead to the same light.

February 03 – Makam Nakshatra, Yati Puja & Maha Magha Amrita Snanam

The Final Immersion into Immortality

The full moon in Makam (Magham) Nakshatra gives the month its name—*Magha*, revered by Acharyas as the holiest of months.

Yati Puja

Every lineage in Bharat traces itself to a sage. Honoring sannyasis is honoring the living backbone of Dharma. On this day, saints are worshipped as embodiments of renunciation and wisdom.

Maha Magham Amrita Snanam

This final holy bath is the nectar dip—the culmination of all rituals. It symbolizes rebirth, closure, and return. The pilgrim leaves not as they arrived, but renewed, anchored, and illumined.

Conclusion

From silence to celebration, from secrecy to splendor, the Maha Magha Mahotsavam unfolds as a living scripture on the banks of the Bharathapuzha. Each day is a step inward, and the final immersion is not merely into water—but into remembrance, continuity, and eternal Dharma.

IMPORTANT DATES (SNAN/BATHING DAYS)

(January 18, 2026–February 3, 2026)

Jan 18 (Sunday): Mauni Amavasya (The most sacred bathing day; observance of silence).

Jan 19 (Monday): Dharma Dhwajarohanam (Flag Hoisting) & Commencement of Magha Gupta Navaratri.

Jan 22 (Thursday): Ganesh Jayanti & Arrival of the Mahameru Rath Yatra.

Jan 23 (Friday): Vasant Panchami (Worship of Goddess Saraswati).

Jan 25 (Sunday): Ratha Saptami (Worship of the Sun God/ Navagrahas).

Jan 26 (Monday): Bhishma Ashtami.

Feb 1 (Sunday): Magha Purnima / Thaipooyam (Major Royal Bath).

Feb 3 (Tuesday): Maha Magham Amritasnanam (final concluding holy dip) & closing ceremony.

BOOKS BY THIS AUTHOR

1. Where Can You Find Salvation? Who Will Bless You With Salvation When Your Life Journey Ends? (Kasi, The Moksha Nagari)

The book 'Where Can You Find Salvation? Who will grant you with salvation at the end of your life's journey?' 'Kasi, the Moksha Nagari,' serves as a spiritual guide for both followers of Lord Siva and those seeking liberation (Mukti) and salvation in the holy city of Kasi. Kasi, recognized as one of the world's holiest cities, has unparalleled spiritual significance as a manifestation of the deity Lord Siva. The divine Ganga flowing through its heart purifies everyone who visits Kasi and its banks. People claim to locate Kasi on Lord Siva's trident and to radiate eternal happiness. Kasi's purity surpasses humanity, bringing salvation to all living beings, including humans, animals, birds, and insects. Every breath you take in Kasi is sacred, every sound is holy, and each step brings us closer to moksha (salvation) from the never-ending cycle of birth, death, and rebirth in Samsara. Kasi is more than just a destination for pilgrims and spiritual seekers. People widely recognize Kasi as the city of salvation. Kasi provides a spiritual haven where dedication and heavenly grace come together to guide every soul to liberty from samsara.

2. Mystics Of The Maha Kumbh (Prayag Raj Purna Kumbh Mela)

The book 'Mystics of the Maha Kumbh' (Prayag Raj Purna

Kumbh Mela) immerses readers in a global religious gathering. It discusses the Maha Kumbh's shifting surroundings, religious ceremonies, and profound spiritual practices. The book primarily tells the personal experiences of devotees, saints, and seekers who gather to celebrate faith and dedication. The plot revolves around Akharas, which are medieval monastic societies, and the enigmatic Naga Sadhus, who abandon their everyday lives to become spiritually aware. It also addresses lesser-known spiritual gurus whose expertise and simplicity have a significant impact on those looking for spiritual awakening.

The book goes into esoteric practices, meditation techniques, and lessons that can transform your life. It demonstrates how critical it is to preserve India's rich spiritual tradition and apply its timeless principles in contemporary life.

'Mystics of the Maha Kumbh' investigates those who spend their entire lives attempting to solve life's riddles. It honors religion's strength and the universal longing for self-realization. We aim to motivate readers by imparting the wisdom and enchantment of this unique occasion.

3. Philosophical Teachings & Commandments Of Lord Dattatreya (Shri Kshetra Ganagapur)

The book 'Philosophical Teachings and Commandments of Lord Dattatreya,' (Shri Kshetra Ganagapur) dives deeply into Lord Dattatreya's timeless wisdom, which represents the Trimurti of Brahma, Vishnu, and Shiva. Lord Dattatreya, the eternal teacher, guides seekers to enlightenment with lectures on simplicity, self-realization, and harmonious living, with a focus on the famous pilgrimage destination of Shri Kshetra Ganagapur. The book delves deeply into his philosophical beliefs on Advaita Vedanta (non-dualism), detachment, and the synthesis of knowledge, devotion, and action, encouraging readers to seek inner peace, discipline, and spiritual fulfillment. Lord

Dattatreya emphasizes the interconnectivity of creation by drawing lessons from 24 Gurus, including natural components and sentient beings. He highlights the connection between the individual soul (Atman) and the Supreme Consciousness (Brahman), emphasizing the significance of conquering ego and duality in order to obtain liberation.

Dattatreya's teachings emphasize wisdom, compassion, universal brotherhood, and cosmic order, laying the groundwork for spiritual growth. Rituals, festivals, and sacred monuments enhance devotees' faiths at Shri Kshetra Ganagapur, a transforming sanctuary of healing and spiritual energy. Lord Dattatreya's ageless teachings provide practical guidance for overcoming challenges, improving self-awareness, and nurturing inner peace. This comprehensive spiritual handbook encourages simplicity, compassion, and a deep connection to the divine.

4. Maha Kumbh: A Scientific Treasure Trove: (Maha Kumbh A Haven For Scientists)

This book, "Maha Kumbh: A Scientific Treasure Trove," offers a unique viewpoint on the Maha Kumbh Mela. It highlights the festival's potential as a world-class scientific laboratory, transcending its religious and cultural roots. This innovative technique sets it apart from previous Maha Kumbh works and provides a riveting analysis of the festival's many facets.

Unveiling Living Laboratory:

The book explores Maha Kumbh's living laboratory, showing its potential for revolutionary study across fields. It painstakingly analyses the festival's distinctive qualities that make it a significant scientific resource. The vast assembly of millions, the temporary mega-city, and the powerful spiritual atmosphere form a dynamic setting for exploration.

The book promotes an interdisciplinary approach to understanding the Maha Kumbh, connecting spirituality and science. It examines the festival's potential for public health, sociology, psychology, and environmental science study. With insights from these many fields, the book provides a comprehensive view of the festival's intricacies and linkages.

The book explores real-world applications of research undertaken during the Maha Kumbh, going beyond theoretical investigation. It shows how the festival's unique setting might aid long-term growth and comprehension of massive crowds. Studying crowd dynamics, public health management, and environmental sustainability during the Kumbh Mela may enhance the planning and administration of future major events.

A stimulus for scientific discovery: The book inspires scientists and researchers to regard the Maha Kumbh as a place of significant discoveries. It stresses the importance of multidisciplinary teamwork and cross-cultural understanding to maximise the festival's scientific potential. The book encourages scientists to explore new horizons and improve our knowledge of human behaviour, societal dynamics, religion, and science by highlighting Kumbh Mela's numerous study potentials.

The book explores unknown scientific realms in the Maha Kumbh, answering key issues about the event. Faith and health: how spiritual activities affect physical and mental health. It also examines the festival's environmental effect and creative sustainability measures. The book explores these undiscovered realms to better comprehend the Maha Kumbh and its potential to advance science and human welfare.

The book "Maha Kumbh: A Scientific Treasure Trove" offers a unique perspective on the Maha Kumbh Mela. It shows the festival's scientific potential beyond its religious and cultural image. The book gives a new and incisive look at the Maha Kumbh by highlighting the festival's multidisciplinary research, real-world applications, and potential for revolutionary discoveries. The book inspires scientists, scholars, and the public to see the festival's diversity and spiritual and scientific value.

5. Transform Your Leadership: Modern Administrative Secrets From The Epics: (A Holistic Guide Through The Mahabharata, Ramayana, And Bhagavatam)

Transform Your Leadership: Modern Administrative Secrets from The Epics: (A Holistic Guide Through the Mahabharata, Ramayana, and Bhagavatam) offers a refreshing take on leadership by blending ancient Indian wisdom with today's management challenges. Drawing deeply from the Mahabharata, Ramayana, and Srimad Bhagavatam, the book unlocks timeless strategies for ethical decision-making, people-centric governance, and spiritually rooted leadership.

Rather than focusing solely on material goals, it encourages a broader vision—one that values inner growth, strong relationships, and purposeful action. From Krishna's strategic insights and Rama's integrity to the Bhagavatam's emphasis on self-awareness, the narrative provides transformative lessons that speak to leaders across generations.

Through rich storytelling and real-world parallels, this guide inspires leaders to lead with wisdom, balance, and heart, creating a legacy of both excellence and meaning.

In essence, the book provides a practical guide for modern leaders to cultivate ethical, compassionate, and spiritually aware leadership by drawing upon the rich wisdom of India's ancient epics, enabling them to navigate complex challenges and create a lasting positive impact.

6. Kashi Calls (A Journey To Enlightenment)

"Kashi Calls" (A Journey to Enlightenment) is not just a book; it is a divine summons—a call from Kashi that echoes through lifetimes. It embodies the essence of the eternal city, capturing the chants of sadhus, the prayers of seekers, and the soul's longing for liberation. This work is an invocation that bridges the finite and the infinite, urging readers to surrender illusions and embrace the divine.

These pages offer a pilgrimage of the soul—walking the Panchkroshi Yatra, feeling the cold touch of the Ganga at dawn, and encountering the silent gaze of Kaal Bhairav. The book brings Kashi's rituals, legends, and truths to life, immersing readers in a visceral experience.

"Kashi Calls" reflects the seeker's soul, asking:

1. Have you ever felt drawn to a place you have never seen?
2. Has the Ganga Aarti awakened a forgotten prayer within you?
3. Does the smoke from Manikarnika whisper of liberation instead of death?

Ancient tales from the Skanda Purana blend seamlessly with modern pilgrim stories—a scientist awed by Jyotirlingas, a grieving widow comforted by Annapurna, and a sceptic transformed by the Dwadasha Aditya temples.

More than a guide, this book is a revelation. It awakens Kashi within, echoing "Har Har Mahadev!" long after the final page. It is a pilgrimage of the soul—open it, and Kashi will open you.

7. The Guru's Advaitamrutam

"The Guru's Advitamrutam" distinguishes itself as more than just a spiritual text; it is a unique guide for profound inner transformation. Its main strength is its practical retreat format, which provides a clear, step-by-step path to truly understanding Advaita Vedanta, instead of just learning the theory. This hands-on approach directly addresses modern longings for deeper meaning.

The book excels in the experiential application of Advaita. It does not just explain concepts like Maya or Viveka; it guides readers on how to live them, integrating ancient principles like Sadhana Chatushtayam, Shravana, Manana, and Nididhyasana into daily routines. It adopts a holistic approach, providing practical strategies for mind control (e.g., pranayama, mantra) and guidance on overcoming emotional blocks, recognising the realistic challenges spiritual seekers face.

Ultimately, its focus is on self-realisation (Brahmatman Aikyam) and living liberated. The book meticulously describes this direct experience of unity, outlining the characteristics of a jivanmukta and guiding readers to live purposefully, rooted in Advaitic truth. The title itself, "Advitamrutam" (nectar of Advaita), embodies its promise: a life-transforming essence leading to liberation and spiritual immortality. This makes the book a guided, practical, and holistic pathway to experiencing the liberating truth of Advaita Vedanta for contemporary seekers

8. Daivī Śakti In You: Thyself The Power (Discovering The Divine Energy That Drives The Cosmos And The Self)

'Daivī Śakti in You: Thyself, The Power' explores the driving force behind all activities. Starting with the age-old question, "You know your birth, but when was energy born?" This study takes the reader beyond the material and mental realms to the Divine Power that created everything, sustains our planet, and illuminates us. This study posits that power derives from the movement of Śakti, the Infinite Consciousness, rather than from physical strength or control. The Vedas and Upanishads explain this power through the threefold rhythm of creation—thought, purpose, and action. The universe is a living sphere of sacred energy—passing every atom, breath, and heartbeat, from massive galaxies to delicate vibrations.

This book shows that Goddesses Durga, Lakshmi, Saraswati, Kali, and Lalita represent our strength, prosperity, insight, elegance, and bravery. Lords Brahma, Vishnu, and Shiva represent the cycle of life, death, and rebirth in all living things.

Every aspect of consciousness and love is divine, and the book sensitively portrays this. The literature connects spirituality and nature by demonstrating how Prakriti Śakti (five elements, planetary energies, and time) affect human experience. Fire, earth, water, air, and space symbolize divine consciousness. Harmonizing with cosmic energy allows one to live happily with nature and God. Energy vibrations from ideas and emotions shape reality. The phrase "Yad bhāvam, tad bhavati" implies that our consciousness shapes our identity. With concentrated intention, true emotions, and meditation awareness, turn your chaotic mind into a powerful weapon for creating the divine. True mastery of Śakti requires determination, devotion, and self-control. Thereafter, the book reveals mystical powers and dormant energy. That power is neutral when driven by love and destructive when motivated by ego. Humble and self-regenerate seekers use spiritual energy for themselves and others. The reader learns that spiritual energy brings light when used appropriately, but darkness when misused. While power without purity leads to pride, devotion softens strength and transforms the heart into a temple of the Śakti. Fear saps energy, whereas devotion boosts it. Wisdom requires addressing anxieties, trusting, and accepting divine love.

The book concludes with a discussion of Śakti as a daily presence and how to live with it. Finding harmony in one's daily life's divine, natural, mental, and hidden components leads to balance, thriving, and calm, as seen below. A true spiritual existence involves actively participating in the cosmos and thanking the Divine Mother with every breath, moment, and action.

Instead of seeking Śakti, remember its inherent divinity, a timeless reality, as demonstrated in the end. Invoking her with love, clarity, and surrender gives the devotee guidance, strength, calmness, and illumination. The ancient chant states, "Sarvaṁ khalvidaṁ Brahma—All is Brahman." This book invites readers to experience and comprehend heavenly power.

Understanding this reality transforms every heartbeat into a praise hymn and every deed into an expression of Daivī Śakti, the eternal force that sustains the universe and individuals.

9. Beyond The Hero (Heroic Past, Cyborg Future, Wisdom-Centric, Quantum Leadership)

Beyond the Hero (Heroic Past, Cyborg Future, Wisdom-Centric, Quantum Leadership) challenges one of the most enduring assumptions in leadership theory: that progress depends on exceptional individuals. The book argues that hero-centric leadership models—rooted in individual brilliance, charisma, and centralised authority—are structurally incompatible with the complexity, speed, and scale of the digital and AI-mediated age. As cognitive load increasingly exceeds human limits, leadership can no longer rely on personal genius. It must evolve into augmented, distributed, and architected systems of intelligence.

The book begins by dismantling the myth of the heroic leader. It traces the historical foundations of "Great Man" leadership and reveals the hidden fragility of organisations dependent on singular brilliance—systems prone to cognitive overload, bias, succession risk, and catastrophic failure. The contemporary leadership crisis, the book contends, is not a shortage of talent but a failure of system design, where complexity has outpaced individual decision-making capacity.

From this diagnosis, Beyond the Hero introduces the concept of the Cyborg Leader: not a machine replacing human judgment, but a human leader symbiotically integrated with AI, data, and networks. In this model, leadership shifts from command to architecture. Intelligence becomes a property of the system rather than the individual, supported by decision frameworks, data infrastructure, and ethical governance.

Crucially, the book moves leadership discourse from psychology to engineering. It replaces fragile high-potential dependency with an all-potential (All-Po) architecture that democratises leadership capacity across organisations, enhancing resilience and systemic reliability.

The book concludes by situating leadership evolution within a broader civilisational shift—from heroic individualism to collective intelligence and ethical stewardship. Heroic leadership centralised authority; cyborg leadership distributes cognition across human–machine systems; wisdom-centric leadership governs power with ethical foresight, while quantum leadership defines the nonlinear environment that makes this evolution inevitable. Ultimately, Beyond the Hero reframes leadership not as dominance, but as a disciplined practice of responsibility—ensuring that intelligence, however powerful, remains in service of humanity and the living systems upon which it depends.

ABOUT THE AUTHOR

Dr. C S Rayudu

From the sanctified soil of Mallayapalli in Andhra Pradesh arises a voice attuned to the deeper pulse of Bharat's eternal spirit. Dr. C. S. Rayudu is not merely a recorder of sacred traditions, but a devoted sādhaka, whose life has been shaped by the profound samskāras received at the feet of his revered parents, Late Shri Subbanna Garu and Late Srimathi Papamma Garu. Their blessings and lived ideals became the unseen altar upon which his inner journey was ignited—anchoring him firmly in dharma while gently opening his heart to higher inquiry and spiritual realization.

For over four decades, Dr. Rayudu walked the noble path of Vidya Dāna, offering knowledge as a sacred trust rather than a profession. In classrooms transformed into quiet sanctuaries of learning, he awakened young minds not only to intellect but to ethics, character, and responsibility. Teaching for him was a yajña—an unbroken offering of time, patience, and conscience. The Best Teacher awards he received stand not merely as honours, but as gentle affirmations of a life aligned with purpose and service.

Beyond the world of academics, his life unfolds as a pilgrimage of the soul. Drawn irresistibly to India's great spiritual power-centres, he journeyed across the sacred geography of Bharat—Tirumala, Sabarimala, Srisailam, Rameswaram, Kāśī, Shri Kshetra Ganagapur, Mantralayam and other sacred places—absorbing the living presence of each kṣetra into his inner landscape. A luminous moment in this odyssey was his recitation of Śrīmad Bhāgavatam ślokas during Nada Nīrājanam at Tirumala, where his voice merged with the wind beneath the divine gaze of Lord Venkateśvara, sealing his bond with grace beyond words.

From this inner silence and lived devotion arose his literary offerings—books not written to instruct alone, but to awaken remembrance. His works serve as lamps for seekers navigating the paths of mokṣa, bhakti, advaita, and embodied spirituality, including Where Can You Find Salvation?, Philosophical Teachings & Commandments of Lord Dattatreya, Kashi Calls, The Guru's Advaitāmṛtam, Daivī Śakti in You, Mystics of the Maha Kumbh, Maha Kumbh: A Scientific Treasure Trove, Grow Up, Stay Ageless, and Transform Your Leadership. Each text carries the fragrance of lived insight rather than borrowed knowledge.

In his latest work, Return of Maha Magha: The Sacred Kumbh of the South, Dr. Rayudu stands as a bridge between epochs—between memory and renewal, scholarship and surrender. Through the lens of Sage Agastya and the sacred destiny of the Dakṣiṇa, he invites readers to rediscover the South not as a region, but as a civilizational anchor of grace, balance, and preservation.

Blending academic rigor with devotional depth, Dr. C. S. Rayudu continues to illuminate the spiritual majesty of the southern land, offering timeless wisdom to all who seek a life aligned with meaning, harmony, and divine purpose.

EPILOGUE

When the River Remembers Again

The South has always been known as the land of descending grace—the sacred direction where divinity does not withdraw from the world but gently enters it. In the *Dakṣiṇa*, the Divine does not remain distant or ascetic alone; it becomes intimate, embodied, and sustaining. Here, *Śakti* is not a philosophical abstraction but a living presence—felt in yielding soil and sprouting seed, in nourishing rivers and faithful rains, and in the quiet continuity that allows life and civilization to endure. Grace in the South is rarely dramatic; it is patient, rhythmic, and preservative—the grace that carries memory forward across generations.

The North moves to a different rhythm. It is the realm of *Śiva*—of ascent and stillness, of icy peaks and inner silence, of renunciation that lifts consciousness beyond form. The Himalayas rise as a civilizational symbol of transcendence, reminding humanity that liberation lies in withdrawal, restraint, and inward turning. This northern impulse protects civilization from excess, forgetfulness, and the loss of the Absolute.

Civilization remains whole only when these two movements—descent and ascent, *Śakti* and Śiva—remain in sacred dialogue. When ascent alone prevails, life becomes brittle and unrooted; when descent alone dominates, transcendence fades into habit. The health of *Bharatavarṣa* has always depended upon the harmony between these two sacred directions.

The ancient legend of *Sage Agastya* remembers this balance. When gods and sages gathered in the Himalayas for the divine wedding of *Śiva* and *Pārvatī*, the earth itself tilted under the concentrated weight of sanctity. Creation signalled imbalance. To restore equilibrium, Śiva sent Agastya southward —bearing Vedic fire, mantra, and tapas. His journey was not exile but cosmic necessity. By settling in the *Dakṣiṇa*, *Agastya* redistributed spiritual gravity, making the southern land capable once more of receiving, holding, and transmitting grace. Through him, the sacred flowed beyond the heights of the Himalayas, uniting rivers, forests, and peoples into a single, continuous holy field.

Maha Magha in the South stands today as the *Agastya Principle* reborn. It is the *Dakṣiṇa Kumbh*—not an imitation of northern forms, but a complementary axis where *Śakti* is worshipped, *Tantra* finds its natural home, and the sacred is lived rather than withdrawn from. Here, the river does not merely carry water; it carries memory.

Maha Magha is not a spectacle. It does not seek noise or display. It is a quiet remembrance of when to gather, when to bathe, and when to bow before Time. When the *Bharathapuzha* flows in sacred alignment, time itself softens. The river flows, the stars consent, and *Dharma* breathes again through human life.

What has returned is not an event but a rhythm. Not a festival to be consumed, but a vow to be carried forward.

May that yet unborn step into these waters and feel what we have felt.
May the river remember them, as it remembers us.
May *Maha Magha* continue—not in memory alone, but in lived continuity—
until time itself comes again to bathe.

ACKNOWLEDGEMENT

With deepest reverence and gratitude, I offer this acknowledgement to all those who have made the return of '*Maha Magha*' possible—those whose vision, dedication, and devotion restored a sacred rhythm that had slept for centuries.

I bow to the conceivers of the rejuvenation, whose inner conviction saw the possibility of revival when history had rendered silence. Your faith was the seed from which this great movement sprouted.

I thank the organizers and promoters, who transformed aspiration into action with tireless effort, navigating the complexities of time, tradition, and administration. Your service was the living *yajña* that brought the sacred back to the riverbanks.

To the youth, who stepped forward with enthusiasm and discipline, carrying the future of this tradition in their hands—your energy has become the new current of Maha Magha.

To the scholars, who illuminated the deeper meanings through research, texts, and interpretation—your wisdom gave the festival its context and its voice.

To the sages, sadhus, devotees, and spiritual seekers whose hearts remained steadfast in devotion, your presence became the sacred atmosphere in which the tradition could breathe again.

To the institutions and all participating promoters, whose

support preserved and propagated the sanctity of the Keral Kumbh—your commitment ensured that this revival was not merely an event but a lasting movement.

I extend my heartfelt gratitude to my beloved wife, Subhasini, whose unwavering companionship and spiritual support have been my constant strength. Her faith and love have been the silent pillar behind every step of this journey.

To our children—Sushma, Sugun, and Susheel—your patience, encouragement, and understanding have been a blessing beyond measure.

To all the members of my family, whose blessings, support, and prayers have sustained me—your love has been the sacred shelter that allowed this work to come into being.

May this book serve as a humble offering to all of you—an enduring remembrance of the sacred Nile river that flows through time and the tradition that has returned to its rightful home.

Om Tat Sat...

www.ingramcontent.com/pod-product-compliance
Lightning Source LLC
Chambersburg PA
CBHW062135160726
48282CB00027B/836